Why

Marry

Jewish?

Why Marry Jewish?

Surprising Reasons for Jews to Marry Jews

DORON KORNBLUTH

TARGUM/FELDHEIM

First published 2003
Copyright © 2003 by Doron Kornbluth
ISBN 1-56871-250-2

Published by:
TARGUM PRESS, INC.
22700 W. Eleven Mile Rd.
Southfield, MI 48034
E-mail: targum@netvision.net.il
Fax: 888-298-9992
www.targum.com

Distributed by:
FELDHEIM PUBLISHERS
202 Airport Executive Park
Nanuet, NY 10954
www.feldheim.com

Printed in Israel

For organizational and/or volume discounts, or to share your comments
or intermarriage experiences, please e-mail tikvaket@netvision.net.il.

ניתן להשיג הסכמות לספר מהמוציא לאור.

Contents

Appendices

Acknowledgments

When, at the beginning of 2001, the executive directors of the Heritage House in Jerusalem asked me to create an educational package for the intermarriage and assimilation films that they had created, I had little idea what I was getting into. Since then, Rabbis Yirmiyohu Abramov, Avraham Edelstein, and Meir Schuster have become my teachers and role models. In their tireless efforts to help the Jewish people, they gave me permission to incorporate the material that I had gathered for the popular *Love & Legacy Seminar* into this book. While I had previously collected sources and jotted down ideas for an intermarriage book, the seminar research saved me enormous amounts of time and energy. Their part in this publication is immense, and I hope that they are proud of it. Their colleague Rabbi Yaakov Miller has also been instrumental in a variety of ways and I am very grateful.

Mr. Richard Horowitz deserves special thanks. His tireless work on behalf of the Jewish people and generous support of innovative projects such as this one make me proud that he has been a driving force behind this work. May he go from strength to strength.

David and Talya Roth helped me get started in the field. I consider them both friends and colleagues, and remain in their debt.

I hope Dr. Steven Bayme (director of Jewish Communal Affairs of the American Jewish Committee) *sheps naches* from this work. His early encouragement of my research and writing in this area was heartening, and his many publications on intermarriage made my work much easier.

Rabbi Dovid Refson and Rabbi Eliezer Liff have encouraged my teaching and writing, and given valuable suggestions about how to best discuss intermarriage. Their support is much appreciated. Rabbi Y. Berkovits, Rabbi B. Gershonfeld, Rabbi Y. Kamenetzky, Rabbi D. Merling, and Rabbi Y. Rohr have all given excellent advice and practical ideas, and I remain in their debt.

Dr. Lisa Aiken, Rabbi Maccabee Avishur, Brian Bebchik, Dave Behrendt, Mrs. Barbara Bennett, Ariel Bergash, Rabbi J. Bloom, Rabbi Yonason Bressel, Andye Freedman, Mrs. Freyde Freedman, Ian Freedman, Mrs. Allison Fried, Daniel and Lauren Green, Moshe Hamburg, Rabbi J. Hamilton, Rabbi L. Kelemen, Prof. B. Kolbrener, my brother Mark Kornbluth, Yehoshua Looks, Mrs. Lori Palatnik (who gets credit for the title of this book), Rabbi Yigal Segal of the helpful Jewish Literacy Foundation, Rabbi and Mrs. Baruch Yellin, and many others were extremely helpful in commenting on various parts of the manuscript and/or the project as a whole. Each of them will recognize, I hope, some of their wise suggestions implemented in the final version. Personally and professionally, I thank them.

I am grateful to the Targum Press team, especially Rabbi Moshe Dombey for his experience and care, D. Liff for her eye-catching design, and Ita Olesker for her insightful comments.

My in-laws have been extremely helpful in this work and so many other facets of our lives. Their encouragement is much appreciated.

As in all my endeavors, my parents have been extremely supportive during the writing of *Why Marry Jewish?* Their voices echo throughout this book, and their love echoes throughout my life. I am trying not to take them for granted.

Finally comes my wife, Sarah Tikvah. This book could not have been written without her wisdom, patience, and positive attitude. She is last mentioned here, but first in my thoughts.

Doron Kornbluth
Jerusalem
5763 / 2003

Introduction

I don't blame you for being open to intermarriage. It has, after all, become the norm. A clear majority of Jews today marry non-Jews. In fact, the idea of inter-marriage has become so acceptable that to many Jews, anyone who suggests that it may not be such a good idea may easily be considered backwards or racist. In our mod-ern, multicultural world, the real question is not why people are intermarrying, but rather why *not* intermarry?

Interestingly, only a generation or two ago, almost every Jewish leader representing the wide spectrum of voices within the Jewish people argued that intermarriage was bad for the individual and bad for the community. In fact, universal Jewish opposition to intermarriage has its ideological roots as far back as the roots of Judaism itself. Abraham instructed Eliezer not to find a wife for his son Isaac from the non-Jewish Canaanites.[1] Similarly, Rebecca insisted that her son Jacob not marry the "daughters of the land."[2] The Bible itself warns against in-termarriage with the local nations surrounding the ancient Israelites,[3] and it was one of the main points that the Prophet Ezra emphasized when our ancestors returned to Israel from the Babylonian Exile some 2500 years ago.[4] Furthermore, intermarriage was never regarded as "just another law." It was always seen as particularly tragic: a Jewish parent's worst nightmare.

Considering the new acceptance of intermarriage, we need to ask ourselves: was all of Jewish history and thought wrong?

I've spent hundreds of hours researching the subject of intermarriage. I've pored over statistics, read studies, interviewed experts, read books, listened to tapes, and watched videos. I've spoken with children of intermarriage. Time and time again, I've discussed it with people from diverse backgrounds with various experiences.[5] I've come to the conclusion that people are mistaken when they think that intermarried families live "happily ever after" and that the kids stay Jewish. While it may surprise you — and hence the title of the book — the facts speak for themselves: if you are Jewish, your chances of having a happy marriage, of your kids feeling rooted and stable, and of having Jewish descendants are all significantly higher if you marry another Jew — whether a sincere convert or someone born Jewish.[6]

It is true, statistics don't mean that every single person will experience what the numbers show. After all, there are some drivers who manage to navigate sharp curves at high speeds without needing to slow down. But in intermarriage as well as driving, is it not appropriate to warn people of the inherent risks that they are about to face?

Discussions on intermarriage are far from over. No one should be branded "good" or "bad" Jews — with attacks on Israel and the recent worldwide resurgence of anti-Semitism, we need unity and civility now more than ever. Furthermore, while the majority of rabbis today oppose intermarriage,[7] there is very little information available upon which people can base discussions and conclusions.[8] It is my fervent hope that *Why Marry Jewish?* will help readers make an informed decision on what is arguably one of the most important choices that they will ever make.[9]

Notes

1. Genesis, ch. 24.
2. Genesis, ch. 27.
3. Exodus 34:16 and Deuteronomy 7:3–4.
4. Book of Ezra, ch. 9.
5. Throughout this book, when no source is given for a direct quote, it is taken from these interviews.
6. Throughout this book, it is important to keep in mind that a non-Jew who undergoes a sincere conversion to Judaism (see note 7 below) becomes a full Jew in all respects, and his or her marriage to a born-Jew is not considered an intermarriage at all.
7. A 1999 survey by the Rabbinic Center for Research and Counseling found that a clear majority of rabbis today do not officiate at intermarriages. Orthodox and Conservative rabbis are clearly opposed to intermarriage and do not perform them. Some readers will be surprised that 57% of Reform and Reconstructionist rabbis refuse to perform intermarriages.
8. Aside from various denominational and organizational bro-

chures, only Kalman Packouz's valuable but out-of-print *How To Stop an Intermarriage* deals with the subject. To my knowledge, no other book that speaks directly to Jewish singles themselves is currently available.

9.   Readers will note that this book does not address issues such as (a) "Who is a Jew?" (b) What to do if you are deeply in love with or married to a non-Jew, or (c) If or how synagogues should welcome intermarried families. These issues are important, but should not be confused with the issue that we deal with: an evaluation of the effects of intermarriage itself. Our goal is simply to share information on intermarriage that until now has been unavailable in a modern and accessible format.

Don't Care? Read This

Chapter 1

How Jewish Are You?

You probably agree that an "observant" Jew and a "practicing" Christian shouldn't get married to each other because their marriage and family life will likely be full of struggle and tension. But what if you simply don't care much about being Jewish? Survey after survey indicates that roughly half of the 5.5 million Jews in America today don't even identify their religion as "Judaism" at all and instead choose "no religion" or "other religion."[1] Even some people who do identify themselves as Jews really couldn't care less. Their Jewishness is at best peripheral to their lives.

If you don't care about being Jewish (and your partner doesn't care about being Christian) then it seems like there won't be any marital tension, confused kids, or other issues discussed in this book. Should you then just marry whomever you want?

Therapy Time

It is a good question and an important issue to be dealt with. Let us start with a successful therapy technique that is used around the world with both individuals and groups. You may want to get a pen and paper ready in order to do the exercise yourself.

As you read the words on the following page out loud (or ideally, have someone else read them to you), write down the first word that comes into your mind. Don't think about it — just be honest and jot down your gut reactions. This is what is referred to as a word association exercise. Word associations are very helpful because they access what we really feel, not what our minds have been trained to think. Try to react to each word individually in order to really benefit from the exercise. It is important to take it seriously and let yourself react without any mental evaluation of the words.

Exercises like the one you just did have changed people's lives. Here's why.

Aside from highlighting specific Jewish cultural associations that non-Jewish partners do not share, this exercise reveals that many Jews have innate negative reactions to much Christian imagery and symbolism, while having positive associations with childhood Jewish memories. While most Jewish people may like and respect individual Christians, often they don't much like Christianity and may have heard about what it has done

Jewish Identity Word Association List

Cross

Christmas tree

Star of David

Jesus on the cross

Torah scroll

Gefilte fish

Chuppah

Mezuzah

Menorah

The Pope

The Western Wall

Bar Mitzvah

Jerry Falwell

Pork

Christianity

Passover

Palestinians

Shofar

The Crusades

Louis Farrakhan

Chanukah

Ham

Judaism

Jews for Jesus

Seder

to the Jewish people throughout history. In my experience, the very mention of Christian symbolism evokes
negative feelings among many Jewish people.

Yet what do these same Christian things represent for
Christians? How do they respond to the list? Christian
symbolism has positive associations for non-Jews from
Christian backgrounds, whether or not they are "practicing," for it reminds them of warm childhood memories.

The cross (with or without Jesus on it) is usually the
biggest surprise. Intermarriage therapists recount that
most Christians relate to it as a warm symbol. Many Jews
react to it quite negatively.

> One Jewish husband in a support group for
> intermarried couples surprised even himself
> by using the word "idolatry" as his word as-
> sociation to the word "cross," "fake" for
> next word on the list ("Jesus"), and "mur-
> derers" when confronted with the word
> "Crusaders." His non-Jewish wife re-
> sponded with alarm, crying out, "After four
> years, now I find out what you think of my
> religion? My whole family is Christian! How
> can you say such things — no wonder you
> people get into so much trouble!"
>
> When the husband heard the words
> "you people," he went livid. "You people?
> You're just like your anti-Semitic brother!
> You are the people who have been murder-

ing innocent Jews in the name of Jesus for thousands of years, and you want me to like him? I have some pride! I may have married you but I want nothing to do with Christianity!"

Needless to say, their marriage and future together were in serious jeopardy. Until this encounter, neither realized the extent of their feelings about each other's religion. Because they were in love, they had convinced themselves that they could be happy together. In truth there were serious obstacles in the way. Thankfully, the truth came out before they had children.

Some Jewish educators have a slightly different way of helping people realize their true feelings. They ask simple questions such as: Do you turn your head at the word "Jew" or "Israel"? Will a non-Jewish partner react that way? What is your vision of your future home? Is it more important to you that your kids become rich or stay Jewish? Do you feel a part of history? Whose history? Do you want to be part of the Jewish community? Will your kids be Jewish? Will they be more Jewish than you are? What holidays do you want your children to identify with? Do you imagine your kids getting married in a synagogue or a church? Will your grandchildren be Jewish?

Questions like these emphasize the different priorities and outlooks that many Jews and non-Jews have, and begin an important process of soul-searching.

The point is that whatever backgrounds we come

from, we can be quite unaware of the religious and ethnic loyalties that are deeply embedded within us. There is a lot of stuff going on in our subconscious that we don't know about, and it usually manages to pop up at the worst times, such as emotional life-cycle events and family holidays, thus creating stress, tension, and disagreements. By helping people confront some of the hard questions, exercises like these bring out into the open issues that often remain beneath the surface during the romantic times of falling in love. It is amazing how many couples never discuss fundamental issues such as the ones mentioned in this book until it is too late. And this is a very dangerous omission, for when push comes to shove, most of us are deeply attached to our religious and cultural heritages.

Yeah, but I REALLY Don't Care

What if your answers do not differ substantially from the answers of your non-Jewish friends? True, you may agree that many people are more attached to their heritages than they realize and should therefore marry people with the same heritage that they have. However, what about those who don't really consider themselves particularly Jewish at all no matter what questions you ask them?

This view is not marginal. Today, large numbers of young Jews feel no significant differences from their non-Jewish contemporaries, and rightly so. They went to the same schools and (with the possible exception of a yearly visit to their respective houses of worship) basically lived the same day-to-day lives.

Perhaps most importantly, they watched the same television shows, saw the same movies, and visited the same websites. Mass entertainment and info-tainment have succeeded in creating a unified modern identity even amongst people living in different geographic regions or countries. The university-educated Mongolian with a satellite dish may have more in common with an American of similar age than with his illiterate peasant Mongolian neighbor!

For a large percentage of people, today's main societal influence is television — and its scope is massive. Television is so powerful that it has been accused of creating Western culture. The net effect of all this is that people who live in different countries, people who've never even met, are remarkably similar to each other. All the more so people who grew up in the same country, and whose only differences happened to be their religious backgrounds. There is really very little that separates them. In theory one may agree that different cultural and religious backgrounds may create added difficulties for marriages and families. But let's face it, some will point out, many young people aren't "inter"-marrying — the two partners aren't discernibly different from each other at all![2]

And they are right.

At this stage of their lives, with little knowledge of or interest in their respective backgrounds, the singles in question are extremely similar to each other. Their identities are that of secular Americans, and all the adjectives (Jewish, Christian, etc.) are secondary at best. There really is no problem right now.

But only "right now."

Thinking Long-Term

Jewish tradition explains that one of the signs of wisdom is the ability to foresee the future consequences of present actions[3] — in other words, to think long-term. We all do this at least to some degree. We check periodically with our accountants to ensure that our financial plan is on track, hopefully allowing for a comfortable retirement. We exercise, or at least recognize that we should, in order to stay healthy now and avoid serious problems later in life. And, in the last thirty years or so, our societies have begun to wake up to the long-term effects of poor environmental practices.

However, on the whole, our world moves quickly. We eat fast food and expect fast computers and Internet connections. We switch cities, switch jobs, and some people even switch spouses at a rate never before seen in the history of the planet. We "live in the moment," and often avoid long-term commitments and responsibilities because we simply have no idea what our lives will be like down the road.

It is easy to think short-term, but it leads to problems in all spheres of life. We apply band-aid solutions (because they seem to work in the short-term) and never get to the real issues. The problems thus get worse and worse. Since

we don't contemplate future situations, we find ourselves unprepared to deal with them and thus react
poorly. Since we don't think of our long-term goals and
plans for achieving them, we live passively, constantly
being pushed around by outside influences. In the end,
other people and pressures determine much of our lives.

In some of the most important spheres of life — marriage and family — it is rare to find people who think long-
term. People let themselves "fall in love" rather than
thinking about the kind of person that they want to have
a lifelong loving relationship with. The phrase "falling in
love" itself denotes being passive rather than active and
thoughtful.

It is important to train ourselves to think long-term,
to consider what we want to be like in five or ten years.
What influences do we want to affect us and in what circumstances do we want to find ourselves? If we can determine what direction we are likely to head in, we can
prepare for it.

The Jewish Involvement Time Line

Try the following exercise.

Take a piece of paper and make a horizontal time line
of your life starting with birth at the left end and going
well into old age at the right end. Separate the sections by
five or ten year increments, as you prefer, marking the
line. Rising from the left-hand side of the time line, draw a
vertical line to complete the structure of the graph. At the
bottom of this vertical line, write "little or no Jewish in-

volvement" and at the top of the graph, write "lots of Jewish involvement."

JEWISH INVOLVEMENT TIME LINE

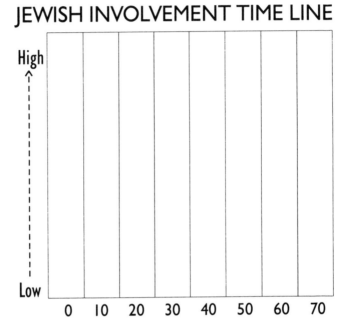

Now that you've made the Jewish Involvement Time Line, proceed to fill it in for yourself and then for a theoretical average Jewish person. At what stages is this person most active? At what stage least active?

Inevitably, in group situations, some people react quickly with a downward sloping line, denoting high Jewish involvement in their childhood (forced Hebrew school, bar and bat mitzvahs), but getting less and less active as the years pass by. The people who suggest this downward sloping time line are usually single, in their twenties. They didn't much enjoy their childhood Jewish involvement and are not particularly sad it is over. They have no plans to get re-involved.

What Goes Down...

These twenty-somethings are somewhat surprised when their slightly older contemporaries attempt to correct the line they've drawn. A more accurate time line, as the thirty-somethings usually convince them, is one that starts high in childhood with some form of regular Jewish education, synagogue attendance, etc. Then, the late teens and early twenties are a time of rebellion and self-discovery. People want to broaden their horizons, "experiment," and gather various experiences. They've often never experienced the meaning and joy of Jewish living, and don't want their "prime years" to be constrained or limited by any external obligations, especially Jewish ones. They therefore correspondingly lower their Jewish involvement to the minimum that their consciences (or their parents!) will allow. The people who draw the downward sloping time line are in this period of their lives, and envision that the downward slope will continue indefinitely.

When people start thinking of settling down, however, their priorities start to change and their Jewish involvement begins to go up. When choosing a neighborhood to live in, it becomes important to know what type of people live there. When their kids are ready, they start thinking of religious school,[4] not because they are "religious," but because they want their kids to feel connected to something, to relate to the concepts of right and wrong, and to hang out with other kids like them. While they may have had complaints about religious school when they were young, they want their kids to share its benefits too. Also, Jewish holidays take on new meaning. They often start out as being observed "for the children," but build into family activities that gain meaning to the parents themselves.

Echoing this thought is Carole Rayburn, a psychologist from Silver Spring, Maryland, with a degree in ministry:

> People with long-dormant beliefs some-
> times have sudden religious awakenings and
> renewed interest in their roots once the kids
> arrive...and at the holidays, it hits them be-
> tween the eyes that they will be responsible
> for the child's religious education and tradi-
> tions.[5]

Renewed interest in one's culture and heritage later in life is not limited to Jewish people. Consider the following interchange on a Greek Orthodox website dealing with the problems of intermarriages:

> *Dear Father,*
>
> *I am a Greek Orthodox Christian and my hus-
> band is Maronite Catholic. While there are many
> similarities between our cultures (he is Lebanese)
> and religions, as you know, they are not the same.
> I am (thank God) pregnant with our first child.
> We discussed the issue of how to baptize our chil-
> dren before we got married. At the time, I agreed*

to allow our children to be Catholic, because I knew what a terribly difficult issue this was for both of us, and believed that as long as our children were good Christians, I could live with them not being Greek Orthodox, as hard as this was for me. It was never an easy issue for us, but I thought I could handle it. Now that the time has come (I am due in December), I am really upset with the situation. I don't know if I can do it.... I feel I am betraying my faith and denying my children something which has been central in my own life and a critical part of my identity.

The counselor on the site responded as follows,

Dear _____ ,

...It is not unusual for one or both partners to have a change of heart after they have made a decision during an earlier period in their relationship. This is both common and understandable. For example, in your case, it is one thing to talk about baptism before marriage, and entirely another thing to actually be carrying a baby and experiencing what you described above....

The point is that feelings about religion and heritage are not constant. More often than not, the time line of religious involvement is not a straight downward line at all. Once families are in the process of being formed, religious and cultural feelings and involvement increase tremendously.

Even when the kids get older and the parents feel less pressure to stay involved in the Jewish community and synagogue, many choose to deepen their involvement for their own benefit. Synagogues are full of people in their forties and older, many of whom were not previously involved in Jewish life. What prompts them to get involved? They may be looking for meaning. When a person feels a need for some form of spiritual expression, it is normal to turn to where they feel most familiar and comfortable, e.g., their parents' places of worship.

Alternatively, a specific event can also spark renewed interest in one's heritage. For instance, most people today still feel that the important life-cycle events such as births, weddings, and deaths should have a religious "feel" to them. The death of parents, for example, has led tens of thousands of Jews to greater involvement in synagogue and Jewish life. They know their parents would want to be buried in a Jewish cemetery and according to Jewish law, and respect their wishes. Jewish mourning practices (e.g., sitting shivah) affect them; the wisdom of our many customs provides comfort and meaning. The year of saying the Kaddish prayer starts out as an obligation, paying one's last respects to one's parent. But as I hear time and time again, it takes on new meaning. Being connected to a synagogue and a Jewish community adds something to the person's life that he or she was lacking, without ever realizing what it was. As one commentator put it:

As they get older, they may find that the
joys of having children, the complexities of
finding work that satisfies them, the sorrow
of losing loved ones, may cause them to feel
a more powerful need for religion than they
could have imagined.... Sometimes, they become involved with a synagogue or church
they thought they'd left behind when they
left home.[6]

Jewish educators have long been aware of the phenomenon of evolving relationships to religion and culture. Since many thirty-something and older Jews get re-
acquainted with their religion and re-integrated into the
Jewish community after long periods of absence, synagogues and other organizations have expanded the adult
education options available to this large and growing
population.

Research in the area has confirmed the anecdotal evidence. Among the key findings of the recent research of
Brandeis University's Dr. Bethamie Horowitz[7] were that
"60% of the people surveyed reported they have experienced changes in their relationship to Judaism over time."
Interestingly, "subjective attachment" — the feeling that
one's Jewishness is important — is either "steadily high
or increasing for 63% of those surveyed."

Significantly, a recent national Gallup poll[8] found that
the *least* religious time in a person's life was usually their
twenties, which not coincidentally corresponds to the

time that they are single and "exploring." However, the poll shows that whatever the religion may be, these same people get more involved in religious and congregational life as they get older.

Timing Is Everything

This chapter has made two main points: (a) we often are unaware of how deep our Jewish feelings really are, and (b) even if one really doesn't feel very Jewish now, it is not unlikely that the feelings will change. While experts are aware of the expected phenomenon of later-in-life involvement in whatever religion and heritage individuals come from, many Jewish singles are almost completely unaware of what they are likely to go through just a few years down the road. As it turns out, *the very same twenty-something Jews who are in the process of choosing to marry non-Jews just happen to be at what is statistically the lowest point of Jewish involvement in their lives.* They haven't experienced the up-turn yet, don't foresee one, and don't think Judaism is "for them." They don't realize that their perspectives are likely to change. Tragically, they are therefore presently in the worst possible position to make the serious long-term decision that they are making. Without realizing it, these twenty-somethings are in fact fully at risk of the common intermarriage problems discussed in subsequent chapters.

Notes

1. The Jewish Identity Survey of 2001 found that there are approximately 5.5 million American adults who are either Jewish by religion or of Jewish parentage and/or upbringing. Yet only 2.8 million, or 51%, say their religion is Jewish. The rest say that they are members of a non-Jewish religion or profess no religion.

2. A similar idea is the so-called inter-faithless marriage, where neither partner practices much of anything.

3. Babylonian Talmud, tractate *Tamid* 32a.

4. Interestingly enough, many parents have an additional reason for sending their kids to Jewish schools and Jewish day schools: these schools almost universally produce higher academic scores in "secular" subjects such as math, science, and English, and experience far fewer incidences of bad influences such as alcohol, drugs, etc.

5. From www.family.go.com.

6. Cowan, *Mixed Blessings*, 129.

7. "Connections and Journeys," reported by the Jewish Telegraphic Agency on June 27, 2001.

8. Poll released to the public on July 14, 1999.

Happy Marriage, Well-Adjusted Kids

Chapter 2

Happily Ever After

Over the last few years, there has been a significant change in the space allocation at most major booksellers: the marriage-improvement sections are constantly getting bigger. Every year, it seems, there are dozens of new titles offering to teach you how to save your marriage. A search on google.com for "good marriages" listed over 398,000 sites! With over half of marriages today ending in divorce, we shouldn't be surprised that people are looking for help. After all, who wants to get divorced?

Indeed, even thirty years ago, the threat of divorce used to scare people so much that it was the most common argument against intermarriage. Jewish parents would quote intermarriages' higher divorce rates. "Intermarriages never last," young people were told. "Get smart before you end up old and alone."

And the facts are undeniably true: divorce rates for couples from different religious backgrounds are considerably higher than when both partners are from the same religious background. While the exact percentages vary with age, location, and a host of other factors, the pattern is true whether the backgrounds in question are Jewish and Christian, Hindu and Muslim, or even Protestant and Catholic. Let us consider only a few of the many studies that verify this phenomenon.

Dr. Larry L. Bumpass and Dr. James A. Sweet researched which factors make marriages more likely to succeed and which factors make them more likely to fail. They concluded that the more *homogamous* the marriage is (meaning the fewer differences the partners have between them) the more likely the marriage is to succeed. While religion was not the only area where differences were problematic (a large divergence in age also created large chances of divorce), it seemed to be the single most problematic area. They stated, "In summary...theories of the role of homogamy in marital stability are supported, particularly for religion."[1]

Professor Howard M. Bahr studied the relationship between interreligious marriages and divorce in Utah and the Mountain States, focusing on the three main Christian denominations in that part of the United States: Catholicism, Protestantism, and Mormonism. His report stated that "Mixed-faith marriages have been shown to have divorce rates several times higher than same-faith marriages...as anticipated, same-faith marriages, whether Mormon-Mormon, Protestant-Protestant, or Catholic-Catholic, have the lowest divorce rates."[2]

Professors Jerry S. Maneker and Robert P. Rankin published findings on the relationship between intermarriage and divorce in marriages involving one Jewish spouse and one non-Jewish spouse. They confirmed the higher divorce rates for marriages with partners from divergent religious backgrounds. Interestingly, they also found that Jews in general have much lower divorce rates than non-Jews. Furthermore, their study rejected the conventional wisdom that intermarriages are only problematic when one or both partners have a strong religious identity. In fact, they found the highest rates of divorce in the cases where neither partner defines him or herself to be "religious"![3]

In 1991, the Council of Jewish Federations National Jewish Population Survey became famous for its revelation of a national intermarriage rate of 52%. Yet that survey also included information on intermarriage and divorce. It found that mixed marriages end in divorce at double the rate of same-faith Jewish marriages.[4]

In 1999, the Creighton University Center for Marriage and Family, in Omaha, Nebraska, researched the relationship between intermarriages and divorce. They found that "The greatest predictor of marital stability for all couples was that they participated in shared religious activities and had fewer religious differences.... Religiously heterogamous marriages have a higher rate of divorce than religiously homogamous marriages." They insightfully concluded: "Religion can bind couples in marriages...or it can be a divisive force in marriages."[5]

Many other researchers[6] have studied the issue and

have confirmed and reconfirmed the fact that when marriage partners hail from different religious backgrounds,
they are taking a significantly greater risk of divorce than if
both partners share a single religious heritage.

Is Love Enough?

Considering the fact that divorce rates are significantly higher for intermarriages than same-religion marriages, you may be surprised to know that most people
aren't particularly concerned about the divorce risk![7]
Why? With the divorce rates being so high anyway, to
most people it seems to matter little whether the percentage is 45%, 50%, 60%, or 65%! Everyone knows that
most marriages end in divorce today, and everyone thinks
and hopes that they will be an exception to the rule,
whether they marry another Jew or not. They hope that
their love will be stronger and they will avoid the pitfalls
that so many others have experienced. So, people con-
clude, the statistics are irrelevant — it all depends on the
individuals involved.

Yet despite the fact that our society's high divorce
rates have caused the anti-intermarriage divorce argument to be less compelling than it once was, we should
consider *why* the divorce rate for intermarried couples is
significantly higher than that of in-married couples. Understanding this phenomenon will help us understand
the major marital challenges facing every intermarriage.

To do this we need to clarify what makes a good marriage. When people are asked about this, some answers

that are given include love, commitment, respect, shared values, closeness, bonding, communication, caring, trust, and understanding.

Whatever factors are listed, note that some of these factors are emotional — a good marriage certainly needs love and romance. And in today's world, Jews fall in love with non-Jews all the time. So this "emotional" part of marriage is not lacking in intermarriage, at least initially.

But is love enough? Over 50% of new marriages today end in divorce. Presumably 99.9% of these couples were "in love" when they got married. From this very point alone, it seems fair to say that early feelings of love are not by themselves enough to sustain a good marriage over the long haul. There needs to be more.

Billy Joel, Christie Brinkley, and Geography

Let us try to focus on other qualities that have been found to be at the foundation of good marriages. They are often referred to as practical or sustaining factors. Take for instance the marriage of musician Billy Joel and supermodel Christie Brinkley. It only lasted a few years. When interviewed, he stated that the main problem they had was geographic: he was a New Yorker, loved the city, and couldn't live anywhere else. She was a California girl who didn't like New York. They simply couldn't find a place to live where both were happy or comfortable. When they went back and forth between Los Angeles and New York, one was unhappy at any given time. If they had tried the middle ground of Iowa, both would be unhappy.

This one "geographic problem" invaded their whole lives and destroyed their marriage.

While we shouldn't be naive enough to think that this was the only reason for their divorce (the real reasons are none of our business), this geographic vignette is an excellent illustration of the importance of non-emotional factors in marriage. Another example might be the desire for children: no matter how in love the couple is, when one spouse wants kids and the other doesn't, the marriage has very serious challenges awaiting it down the road. The point is clear: sometimes love simply cannot beat practicality.[8]

The Practical Side of Intermarriage

Let us consider some of the practical problems that intermarriages are known for. Consider the following questions carefully: Who will perform the wedding? Will it occur in a church or a synagogue? What type of neighborhood will you live in and bring your kids up in? Will your spouse be comfortable in the part of town that you prefer? What religious or ethnic symbolism will be in the house? Will there be a mezuzah on the door or a cross on the wall? Will religious or cultural-type literature be prominent on the shelves? Where will the money you give to charity go? Will you or your spouse attend church or synagogue for weekend services or holidays? Will there be any pressure down the road for one partner to convert? Do you want to be buried in a Jewish, Christian, or sectarian cemetery? What clergy should conduct the ceremony? Will you want to (or be allowed to) be buried together? What mourning practices do you want observed for you?

As you probably know, the most famous intermarriage issues concern children. In many cases the non-Jewish partner can be convinced to let a baby boy have a circumcision. But how does one then object to a baptism? Similarly, will there be a christening? What religious school will the kids go to, if any? Will the kids be brought up in one religion or both? Will your kids know how to read Hebrew? Will they know Christian prayers? Will the family celebrate Chanukah? Christmas? What about the other holidays? Will there be a bar/ bat mitzvah? What if the kids start liking one tradition better than the other? How will you feel if your child, watching television or a film, refers to Jews as "them" and not "us"? Perhaps most importantly, what happens if parental feelings on these crucial issues change, as they often do?[9]

All these questions reflect common problems in intermarriages. Literature on the subject refers to these issues as "time bombs," because they don't seem problematic until they blow up a marriage later on.

As one woman put it:

> *Nothing is simple. Where to live, what holidays to celebrate, what food to serve, where to send the kids to religious school — everything is a question. Everything ends in an argument. Things that should bring you closer drive you further apart.*

> *Eventually we just stopped trusting each other,*
> *and that was the beginning of the end.*

Another woman from Philadelphia related the following:

> *My rabbi showed us a movie that the Reform*
> *movement made about intermarriage, where we*
> *witness group therapy sessions of intermarried*
> *couples. It wasn't pretty. One wife describes how*
> *the day their son was born, she mentioned casu-*
> *ally preparations for the circumcision. Her hus-*
> *band objected to doing such a "barbaric ritual."*
> *Pleading, she finally got him to agree, explaining*
> *how important it was to her religion and to her.*
> *"Fine," he answered, "then I'm sure you'll under-*
> *stand why I insist on getting him baptized!" Their*
> *marriage did not look likely to survive. I heard*
> *that the rabbi had to stop showing the movie be-*
> *cause it got too many congregants upset.*

While all marriages have their challenges, intermar-riages are particularly problematic because the issues that come along with it are both permanent and ex-tremely sensitive. Indeed, as we've seen, the differences that partners bring with them get more problematic with time. Instead of religious background forming a connec-tion that can help a couple through the rough spots that occur in any relationship, religious differences invariably cause and exacerbate tensions in the marriage.

Rabbi Jacob J. Hecht writes:

Love is essential to a marriage; a loveless
marriage is barren and unstable. But much
more is needed. Marriage represents a bond,
an attempt at social continuity and family
security, a concern for the past and a hope
for the future. That bond must be cemented
not only with love, but also with commonality of purpose and a sharing of goals and ideals. Marriage between two people [raised in]
different faiths robs that bond of much of its
commonality.[10]

Who Is Happier?

We have seen that divergent religious and cultural
heritages pose serious challenges to intermarried couples
and lead to significantly higher rates of divorce. We have
also discussed that while feelings of love are almost always present in an intermarriage, added practical challenges make divorce much more common. In fact, even in
cases that do not result in divorce, research in the field
has concluded that intermarriages have more problems
and less happy partners than same-faith marriages.[11] Let
us consider a few of the studies on the subject.

The first serious research of its kind was done by Professor Judson T. Landis in 1949.[12] He studied 4,108 Christian marriages, comparing those where both spouses
were either Catholic or Protestant to those with one
Catholic partner and one Protestant partner. In his land-

mark and widely cited study, Landis concluded:

> Marriages between Catholics and Protes-
> tants entail more hazards than do those be-
> tween members of one faith. Although
> couples discuss before marriage the prob-
> lems arising from religious differences, they
> can find no final solution to the problems
> and the differences do not usually decrease
> with the passing of time after marriage.

Dr. Tim B. Heaton of Brigham Young University ana-
lyzed data from the National Opinion Research Center
(NORC) General Survey of 1982, and summarized that
"results indicate that [religiously] homogamous marriages are more satisfying…religiously homogamous
marriages are characterized by greater marital happiness
than are heterogamous marriages." He also found that
while "the religious identification of children is a major
source of strain in heterogamous marriages…the conflict
over appropriate religious values for children does not account for lower satisfaction."[13] In other words, kids are
not the only problem: even childless intermarried couples
report less marital happiness than childless same-faith
couples.

In 1990, working with Dr. Edith L. Pratt, Professor
Heaton replicated his earlier findings. They wrote, "As was
the case in previous studies, couples of the same denominational affiliation were more likely to have a happy, stable
marriage than those whose religions were different."[14]

In 2000, commenting on the publication of his book, *Should We Stay Together?* Dr. Jeffry Larson, professor and director of Marriage and Family Therapy graduate programs at Brigham Young University, warned of problematic areas that rip marriages apart. Religious differences are among the most dangerous. Despite the old wisdom that opposites attract, he strongly advises against such relationships. "It makes marriage interesting," he says, "but difficult."[15]

Spousal Resentment

In light of these studies showing the lower marital satisfaction rates of intermarriages, it is important to try and gain some insight into why this happens. We have already discussed how love is not enough in the long run, and how arguments and tensions over how to live and how to raise the children are the most common causes of divorce and unhappiness. One reason as yet unmentioned is resentment. One recent study found that "many non-Jewish parents eventually grew to resent their children's Jewish upbringing, though they initially had agreed to the concept. The resentment stemmed from a feeling of exclusion — particularly when the child learned unfamiliar rituals and language."[16]

When this happens, the marriage and the whole family unity are in serious trouble. Consider this account from one non-Jewish woman in New York married to a Jewish man:

> *I don't consider myself much of a Christian, but
> I'm definitely not Jewish like my husband. And I
> dread when his holidays come up — they have
> nothing to do with me and only make me feel like
> a stranger in my own home. Why did he marry me
> if this stuff was so important to him? Why can't
> he just drop the whole thing? It's not fair that he
> has this connection to the kids that I don't.*

Similarly, a non-Jewish Texan married to a Jewish woman remarked:

> *Things were happening in the family that had
> nothing to do with me. I felt, as someone put it,
> as though a ship was slowly leaving the dock and
> I wasn't on board.*

Dr. Sylvia Barack Fishman's 2001 study revealed that these feelings of resentment are far from rare. Referring to non-Jews married to Jews, Dr. Barack Fishman writes:

> Many grew to resent being "shut out" of im-
> portant aspects of their children's lives. Few
> of them wanted to learn Hebrew — some
> had tried! — but they disliked the fact that
> their children were learning a language that
> they did not know. Since they no doubt
> would not have had the same resentful feel-
> ings about their children learning French,
> Spanish, or Italian, it is clear that in these
> cases Hebrew has attained a symbolic sa-
> lience, and may represent the whole package

of religious dislocation that they feel but do
not often articulate.[17]

Marital problems are in fact caused in a variety of
ways. Consider these thoughts of an intermarried Jewish
woman from Australia:

> I spend my life walking on eggshells. I want my
> kids to feel Jewish, but need to hide everything
> from [my husband] or he sulks and gets angry. I
> try and bring in books and videos, but it creates
> major problems between us. It is a struggle. And
> it is very uncomfortable. This one issue is souring
> our entire marriage.

To quote the words of "Jane" in the Reform move-
ment's 1970s film about intermarriage ("When Love
meets Tradition"):

> A lot of these issues are becoming more important
> to me as I grow older, and also now that I'm a
> mother. And it IS an issue. It became an issue the
> first week Bobby was born.

Finally, this last account is from an intermarried Jewish man from Paris:

> We celebrate both religions and so certain times
> of year become very difficult. In December we try
> to outdo each other. Same in the spring for Pass-
> over and Easter. During the High Holidays, she
> tends to disappear and "feel weak" quite often.
> During all these times, my wife and I hardly speak

*to each other in any meaningful way. I even no-
tice her stiffen up whenever Israel is mentioned on
the news, as if she wishes the whole "Jewish
thing" would just disappear. This is not the closeness of marriage that my parents had, or that either of us wanted.* [18]

In these cases and many more like them, we begin to
get a sense of how specific points of disagreement will eat
away at a marriage and eventually threaten its founda-
tions. Furthermore, there are many more points of disagreement than people imagine. Researchers Drs. Evelyn
Lehrer and Carmel Chiswick noted:

Religion also influences many activities beyond the purely religious sphere, including
the education and upbringing of children,
the allocation of time and money, the culti-
vation of social relationships, the development of business and professional
networks, and even the choice of place of
residence. [19]

Researchers Heaton and Pratt echoed this idea in saying that:

Religious orientations may come into play
when deciding about leisure activity,
childrearing, spending money, and many
other facets of marital interaction. Common
religious orientation may also create a more
integrated social network. [20]

No wonder that one child of intermarriage remarked,

> *My parents met in college and didn't think they were that different. But as they got older, their differences became more and more obvious. My father's role modeling had taught him to look forward to one kind of lifestyle, while my mother's role modeling was quite different. They stayed married and never openly fought, but on a whole host of issues — some of them seemingly nothing to do with religion — they always had to compromise and felt uncomfortable with their decisions. Neither achieved the happiness they sought and this was painfully obvious to their children.*

Reports from the Web

In the 1970s and 1980s, as multiculturalism flourished, the conclusions shared above were not widely carried in the popular press. The fact that intermarriage brings with it a host of problems was often known only to those in the field and those who went through the experience themselves. However, the media has recently become aware of the difficulties of intermarriages, citing experts, studies, and even some of the more famous cases of intermarriages gone awry. Consider this tabloid news flash from About.com, which appeared on February 7, 2001:

> Tom Cruise has filed for divorce from Nicole Kidman. He went to court today in Los Angeles and filed on the grounds of irreconcil-

able differences. While it was stated that the separation and divorce were based on their career differences, it is speculated that religious differences are the root of the problem. It seems that Kidman wants their children raised Catholic, and Cruise, a member of the Church of Scientology, is not in agreement with that. The *New York Post* reported that Cruise and the church attempted to save the marriage and Cruise underwent counseling by church leaders, but to no avail. Kidman has been quoted in the past as saying she was, "...still a Catholic girl. It will always stay with you."

In the last few years, the Web has become an impressive repository of reflections on intermarriages. Numerous chat rooms and discussion groups deal with the subject, essentially sharing advice on how to deal with the myriad problems encountered in intermarriages. Consider the following typical example:

From: Religious Skeptic
Subject: Inter-faith Marriages

When my wife and I married at a very young age, I naively thought that our religious differences didn't matter. I've finally realized that it DOES matter to me and am having trouble raising our children in "her" church when I don't support it or many of its doctrines.

And these messages from a different chat room:

As a person who has first-hand experience, I would advise people to marry in their own religion...consider all the problems, right from what they would name their child, how they would raise the child, and also what rituals they would like to follow. And even if it sounds gross I would suggest they should discuss how they would like to be buried/cremated when they die. When young people fall in love they cannot see beyond that and when reality strikes they cannot withstand it and that's why all these divorces take place.

"Hi _____,

I am not sure about the success rates but amongst the many I have seen, I would say [interfaith marriage] is not as successful as the marriages between same religions. There is a lot of guilt, pain, and misery within. Every marriage needs adjustments but intermarriages need adjustments that are likely to change the person's identity. No matter how we deny it in the name of liberalism, religion forms a big part of our identity.... Marriage is not simply a union of two people, it is a union or coming together of two families — not only in the material/literal sense but also in the make-up of the person you are marrying....

And finally, from an anonymous female writer in love

with a man with a different religious background:

> *Hey Lost, I am in the same situation...but I don't*
> *think that it's worth putting myself, his and my*
> *family, and our future children through all the*
> *pain, conflict, and complications....*

The Greek Orthodox Experience

In 2000, Greek Orthodox Priest Reverend Dr. Father Charles Joanides completed a comprehensive study of 160 interfaith spouses in seventeen focus groups for the greater New York Archdiocesan District of the Greek Orthodox Church. As a minority Christian group in the United States, the Greek Orthodox Church has been plagued by its younger members marrying out, mostly with Roman Catholics and Protestants. Reverend Joanides' survey, "The Interfaith Marriage Challenge,"[21] has found wide distribution amongst his own clergy because of its depth and clarity. Its lessons, however, are instructive for any intermarriage situation.

Reverend Joanides described one couple, John (twenty-nine years old) and Jenny (twenty-eight years old) as typical of the intermarried profile among young, educated Greek Orthodox Americans. John was a second-generation Greek Orthodox Christian American, and Mary was a first-generation Hispanic Catholic American. He summarized the couple's situation as follows:

> Some distance lingered between both
> spouses, and both partners learned not to

discuss their religious differences because their discussions would end in heated arguments that appeared…irreconcilable. Their two children were both baptized in the Greek Orthodox Church, they hardly attended liturgy because John was always working and Mary did not feel comfortable in the Greek Orthodox Church. Mary's parents and John continued to have a civil but distant relationship, and vice versa, which periodically flared into arguments. And these tensions lingered for many — nearly ten — years, with no end in sight.

His report emphasizes that struggles related to religious and/or cultural differences were repeatedly mentioned by respondents. In most instances one partner reported feeling that his or her religious and spiritual needs were not being fulfilled since he or she had compromised by agreeing to worship in the partner's church.

Interpersonal guilt was another significant finding: "A typical example that spouses reported were the guilty feelings that these couples experienced when they could not please both sides of their extended families as a result of their decision to worship in either an Orthodox church or non-Orthodox church." He also reported that the separation between some couples was sometimes perceived as "unbridgeable."

The fact that different religious backgrounds create

distance between partners is a constant theme in discussions with intermarried couples. Consider the following statements by two people in intermarriages:

> *It does seem a paradox — wanting to be close to your partner, yet wanting separateness in holding on to your own religion...it is jarring.*

> *Sadly, the reality is that she doesn't and can't understand an important part of me.*

Conclusions

Contributing to a website designed to help intermarried couples work through their myriad problems, one Reform rabbi wrote of his many experiences in this area and noted that intermarriages are far more problematic, unhappy, and divorce-prone than people realize. He also pointed out:

• Many couples, hoping that "somehow things will work" or that "one partner will change," will marry "despite clear danger signs. Some intermarrying individuals don't want to rock the boat, and therefore don't convey their honest feelings to their partners. They may fear losing a partner if they are too demanding about their wishes."

• Today, same-faith marriages have a high risk of divorce. When you add in differences in family backgrounds and traditions, the risk of divorce goes up.

- In addition to the effects on the children themselves, child-related intermarriage tensions are "perhaps the most frequent reason for the failure of an intermarriage." What was agreed to in theory can quickly become a source of great anxiety as a parent holds an infant in his or her arms. Suddenly a promise made years earlier to have children identified and educated as Jews (or Catholics, etc.), is no longer as simple as it once seemed. Many couples rather naively feel that promises made early on in a relationship are cast in stone. In reality, people and circumstances change in the course of life.

In this chapter we have seen that intermarriages are far less successful than people realize. The divorce rate today demonstrates that love is not enough to sustain a happy marriage in the long term. The reality is that marriage is not easy and love can fade if not properly nurtured. It needs help to survive. Common backgrounds, goals, and values are necessary as well. Since many of these are absent in intermarriages, it is not surprising that aside from having significantly higher levels of divorce, intermarried couples report less marital happiness and face many more challenges than same-faith marriages.

From all these studies, experiences, and anecdotes about intermarriages, we can imagine what same-faith marriage can offer. Having only one religion in a marriage is a unique opportunity to "share on every level of life and spirit." By having this common bond with your spouse, all doors are open to growth, comfort, and self-expression no matter what direction you go in. While marrying another Jew is no guarantee of a close, meaningful relationship, it does make achieving such a bond much more likely. Such a marriage gives a framework of holiday and life-cycle events that can help bring a couple closer as the years go on. It gives a sense of the past that together you can build into the future. No matter how "practicing" you may or may not be, marrying someone from your own religious background contributes to a profound sense of togetherness.

Notes

1. Larry L. Bumpass and James A. Sweet, "Differentials in Marital Instability: 1970," *American Sociological Review* 37 (1972): 754–66.

2. Howard M. Bahr in "Religious Intermarriage and Divorce in Utah and the Mountain States," *Journal for the Scientific Study of Religion* 20 (1981): 251–61.

3. Jerry S. Maneker and Robert P. Rankin, "Religious Affiliation and Marital Duration among Those Who File for Divorce in California, 1966–71," *Journal of Divorce and Remarriage* 15 (1991): 205–17.

4. See Phillips, *Re-examining Intermarriage*, 65, table 2-8, which is based directly on 1991 data. Their numbers refer to a 30% divorce rate for intermarrieds and a 16% divorce rate for in-married Jews. Authors of the study caution, "These divorce rates are underestimates, since divorced persons were underrepresented in 1993 [survey on mixed marriage]. Jews who were divorced in 1990 were the most likely to have moved by 1993 and thus were less likely to be reached and interviewed."

    For our purposes, however, it is the comparison between the divorce rates of intermarrieds and in-marrieds that is crucial, not the exact numbers. Because there are so many variables involved, I have shied away from using exact numbers. The fact that intermarriages have significantly higher divorce rates than same-faith marriages is consistent throughout all studies.

5. *Ministry to Interchurch Marriages: A Summary Report*, Creighton University Center for Marriage and Family, Omaha, 1999.

6. Aside from those listed above, interested readers are referred to the following studies, each of which confirms significantly higher divorce rates for intermarriages than same-faith marriages:

Robert Michael, "Determinants of Divorce," in *Sociological Economics*, ed. Louis Devy Garboua (London: SAGE Publications, 1979), 223–54.

Allen S. Mailer, "Reducing the Risks of Divorce: A Responsibility of Religious Educators," *Religious Education* 87 (1992): 471–78.

Evelyn L. Lehrer and Carmel U. Chiswick, "Religion as a Determinant of Marital Stability," *Demography* 30 (1993): 385–404.

Larry L. Bumpass, Teresa Castro Martin, and James A. Sweet, "Background and Early Marital Factors in Marital Disruption" (NSFH Working Paper, no. 14), Center for Demography and Ecology, University of Wisconsin, Madison, 1989.

S. Kenneth Chi and Sharon K. Houseknecht, "Protestant Fundamentalism and Marital Success: A Comparative Approach," *Sociology and Social Research* 69 (1985): 351–74.

Also, each of these studies refers to other studies (not listed here), which all confirm the intermarriage-divorce relationship.

7. Although it is true that fear of divorce may be one of the factors causing people to postpone marriage longer than used to be the case.

8. A well-known Gallup poll from 1989 showed that 57% of divorces were attributed to "incompatibility or arguments over money, family, or children." Quoted in McManus, *Marriage Savers*, 123.

9.   See previous chapter.

10.   Cited in an Ask-the-Rabbi e-mail from www.ohr.edu, July 23, 2000.

11.   Note that adults and children are both at "increased risk for mental and physical problems due to marital distress." (Dr. Scott Stanley, Center for Marital and Family Studies of the University of Denver, paper presented at the Family Impact Seminar, June 1997, Washington, D.C.) Readers are referred to the following studies which document this relationship: Cherlin and Furstenberg, 1994; Coie et al., 1993; Coyne, Kahn, and Gotlib, 1987; Cowan and Cowan, 1992; and Fincham, Grych, and Osborne, 1993.

12.   Judson T. Landis, "Marriages of Mixed and Non-Mixed Religious Faith," *American Sociological Review* 14 (1949): 401–7.

13.   Tim B. Heaton, "Religious Homogamy and Marital Satisfaction Reconsidered," *Journal of Marriage and the Family* 46 (1984): 729–33.

14.   Tim B. Heaton and Edith L. Pratt, "The Effects of Religious Homogamy on Marital Satisfaction and Stability," *Journal of Family Issues* 11 (1990): 204. Other studies include: Bumpass and Sweet, 1972; Burr, 1973; Lewis and Spanier, 1979; Nye and Beraro, 1973; Udry, 1974; and Albrecht et al, 1983.

15.   Larson, *Should We Stay Together?*

16.   Reported on May 3, 2001 by the Jewish Telegraphic Agency. Based on Fishman, "Jewish and Something Else." Dr. Barack Fishman wrote that "non-Jewish spouses raising Jewish children often later found themselves resenting the fact that they had given up their Christmas and other Christian celebrations" (p. 9).

17.   Ibid., 27.

18.   My translation.

19.   Lehrer and Chiswick, "Religion as a Determinant of Marital Stability," 385.

20.   Heaton and Pratt, "Effects of Religious Homogamy," 192.

21.   Published in N.Y. by the Greek Orthodox Church of America, 2000.

Chapter 3

Robert's from France

There is a cute story about a kid who comes home from school one day and asks his father, "Where do I come from?" His father, flustered, starts hemming and hawing, gets red in the face, and eventually mumbles his way through the long prepared explanation of the birds and the bees that he's been dreading for years. When he finishes, the son replies, "No, Dad. I mean where do I come from? Robert says he is from France, and I want to know where I come from."

It is a funny little joke, but it hints at something kids start doing very young and continue through adolescence and beyond – trying to find out who they are and where they fit in. Child psychologists refer to this idea often and assert that even young children need a sense of identity and belonging.

In her workshops, one intermarriage therapist I know of emphasizes the psychological need that kids have for

one clear religious identity. She argues against what is referred to as the dual-religion approach, which is characterized by children growing up with two religions in the
home — "having the best of both worlds." In the first
years of a child's life, intermarried couples often react
negatively to her criticism of this mixed approach. The
parents explain that there really haven't been any problems and question whether her concerns are really an issue for them at all.

From years of experience, this therapist has concluded that these parents indeed have little to worry
about until the child is five or six years old. Young children
aren't bothered by the mixing of religions and in fact seem
to enjoy it — the more presents they receive the better!

But soon after, things get more complicated. Kids
need to feel that they fit in with their friends and the
world around them — which is why they always want
the same toys and clothes as their classmates. When
their friends and playmates ask, "What are you?" they
will often feel embarrassed or uncomfortable for not having a "standard" answer like the other kids. They begin to
ask questions such as "What are we, Jewish or Christian?" and "Do we believe in Jesus?" Beneath the surface,
they are really trying to find out who they are. They may
feel nervous because they don't fully fit in with either
group. They may feel unsure of themselves.

While the "search for self" is a lifelong process, in
childhood and especially adolescence it is very much the
focus of our lives. In these first stages of life, when knowl-

edge, self-confidence, and independence are still relatively weak, children need an extra dose of external support and identification to avoid feeling overwhelmed and alone.

Early feelings of belonging are crucial, because they set up essential psychological and emotional bases that help adults throughout their lives. Through identification with one particular religious and/or cultural community, a child feels part of something, adding immeasurably to his or her self-esteem. Growing up with clarity that one is part of a specific group gives a sense of rootedness and connection with others, the exact thing that so many lonely people in modern societies desperately seek. It gives children one of the greatest gifts that can be given — a sense of confidence and comfort in who they are. It builds the basis for avoiding what has been called the "single greatest source of unhappiness in the modern world": alienation.

C. G. Jung, one of the most important psychoanalysts of the twentieth century, wrote the following:

> I should like to call attention to the following facts. During the past thirty years people from all civilized countries of the earth have consulted me. I have treated many hundreds of patients, the largest number being Protestants, the smaller number Jews, and about five or six believing Catholics. Among all my patients in the second half of life — that is to

say, over thirty-five — there has not been
one whose problem in the last resort was
not that of finding a religious outlook on life.
It is safe to say that every one of them fell ill
because he had lost that which the living religions of every age have given to their followers, and none of them has been really
healed who did not regain his religious outlook.[1]

At first glance, Dr. Jung's comment that people need
a "religious outlook" implies spirituality. And this is certainly true — people need to feel that the world has purpose and that their lives have meaning. Yet the
implications of his comment are wider than that. Included in what he describes is a feeling of belonging, a
sense of self, a knowledge that I am part of something —
in essence, an experience of connectedness with what is
outside of myself.

Human beings today can very easily feel overwhelmed and alienated. In the old country, as they say,
people lived simple lives in small towns. People knew
each other, cared for each other, and relied on each other.
Feeling lost was rarely a danger back then. Today, in our
fast-paced and modern world, we know more and yet
somehow feel less. We can communicate easily with
people around the world but lack the words to forge a
sense of togetherness with our neighbors.

The Jewish Connection[2]

One of the many benefits of identification with the Jewish community is, for the most part, the absence of such a sense of alienation. Jewish life is communally based, to the point that it is difficult to find a prayer that contains the word "I" in it. Judaism itself gives each and every individual a life of historical and communal meaning. With families forming the basic building blocks of community, Jewish life is set up so that no one should feel alone.

For example, in the Diaspora Museum on the grounds of Tel Aviv University in Israel there is a reproduction of a beautiful gold wedding ring that grooms would present to brides. On the ring itself is a model of a miniature house. The idea was that a marriage is not only a union of two individuals, but also the building of a new Jewish home, symbolizing one of the building blocks of the Jewish people. Jewish weddings were and continue to be community celebrations. Oftentimes in Europe and North Africa, the entire community was invited (and came!) for dancing, to say a mazal tov (congratulations), and of course to have something to eat.

The recent resurgence of anti-Semitism has caused many Jews to feel their Jewishness and connect to other Jews. In fact, whether the cause is terrorism in Israel, anti-Semitism in Europe, or financial collapse in Argentina, Jews feel responsible for one another. We help each other. Fundraising, social action, political pressure, prayer, or whatever else possible will be used to aid fellow

Jews, no matter who they are or where they are. Similarly, wherever Jews travel, we are not alone but have immediate connections and, if need be, assistance from the local Jewish community. And even when life is over, the community visits the bereaved and takes care of their needs. In the event that there are no relatives, the representatives of the community ensure a dignified burial according to Jewish tradition. No one is forgotten or abandoned. The entire Jewish life cycle is meant to be lived as part of a community. Feeling oneself to be a full member of a community (rather than having one foot in and one foot out, as in the case of intermarriage) is thus a major advantage, offering commonality and connection, and decreasing aloneness and alienation.[3]

Family Stability and Self-Esteem

Unlike the stability and structure of a home where all members share one religious heritage, when there are competing religions in the home the stability and security of the family itself are weakened. This is a tragic occurrence, for the benefits of growing up in a stable, unified family are manifold.

Recent studies have shown that children in families that maintain a structured and stable family life have fewer emotional problems, have a more positive sense of self, and are able to respond to stressful situations. It was found that children derive a sense of security and a stronger identity from family rituals and from a moderate level of order, regularity, and structure.[4]

Furthermore, low self-esteem is widely seen by psychologists today to be one of the most serious problems facing children and adolescents. Almost without exception, experts in the field of intermarriage mention that kids with a clear religious identity usually have much higher levels of self-esteem than those exhibited by children who come from mixed marriages. Children of intermarriage often lack a clear identity[5] and also the family unity necessary for the development of strong self-esteem. As two experienced commentators put it:

> We talked with many children of intermarriage.... Based on those interviews and our talks with professionals, we have come to feel it is not satisfactory to raise a child with no group identification, no experience of belonging.... We have also come to the conclusion that children feel more secure if they are brought up in one religion, not two — if they have one clear religious identity...children who don't get a clear message about their religious identity can end up struggling for much of their lives to sort it out.[6]

Consider the following typical account from a Web chat room:

> *Hello Joseph and Rashmi and all the readers,*
>
> *This is sunshine again...I am a product of such a marriage, a Hindu-Muslim one.... It has been very, very hard in spite of my parents being very edu-*

*cated and balanced type of people. They have
now been married thirty-one years, which is truly
commendable, and though it would be called a
success story, I believe that they have gone
through so much and sacrificed so much that it
makes me wonder whether it was worth it.... I for
one never knew where I belonged.... Both my parents did not convert, but my mother did give up
practicing her religion more because she wasn't
too religious and she didn't care so we were
brought up in my father's religion. The whole situation just keeps bothering you all your life. I have
always felt kind of a misfit.... You keep asking
questions to yourself as to where you belong,
where do your loyalties stand....*

Marginal Man

In 1937, respected American sociologist Everett
Stonequist created the term "marginal man," referring to
the type of person who lives simultaneously in two cultures, without fully belonging to either. Common personality traits of such "marginal men" are anxiety and
insecurity.

This idea applies well to children of intermarriage today. One of the main subjects discussed at interfaith
counseling workshops[7] is the subject of identity crisis. It
is not easy to have a clear, stable identity when one
grows up the product of an intermarriage. Consider a few

possible scenarios: Daddy always gets tense and stressed when December rolls around. Mommy stands politely at the lighting of the Chanukah candles, but the kids sense her disquiet at what remains to her a "foreign ritual." One set of grandparents has a Christmas tree and gives them Christmas presents. The other has a Chanukah menorah and tries to avoid being "outdone" by the Christmas season. One parent emphasizes Easter, the other Passover. One parent wants the child to stay close to home and hang out with the neighborhood kids. The other parent will drive across town to let the kids spend an hour with their few Jewish friends.

Whatever the particular situation, the truth is that it's very difficult for *any* child or adolescent trying to forge an identity in a confusing world. In the case of children of intermarriages things are generally much harder. It is all too easy for them to feel "neither here nor there," pulled in two opposite directions, innocent bystanders caught in the middle of struggle with no end in sight.

As one college-age product of an intermarriage confessed: "Sometimes I get the sense that I have a foot in each territory and I'm not a citizen of either."

Another child of intermarriage similarly related: "All my life I've been aware of being half-and-half. I feel like I'm on the fringes of things in a lot of ways...there are a whole lot of ways I don't belong. I've wanted to know who I was ever since I was a teenager."

Family Dynamics

Cultural and religious identities aside, intermarriage also risks harming the family dynamic:

> For children of two-religion or no-religion homes, religious identity becomes intertwined with family dynamics. On a conscious or sub-conscious level, they may feel that to embrace one religion means rejecting the parent of the other religion. Even young children feel the pressure of the loyalty dilemma. We asked one little girl whether she liked Christmas or Hanukkah better. "Christmas," she said, but then her eyes widened in alarm. "You promise you won't tell my Daddy that?"[8]

Similarly, one little boy summarized his family's dual religion approach in the following way: "When I do the Jewish stuff, my Dad gets upset. And when I do the Christian stuff, Mom gets angry."

In theory, home is supposed to be a haven, an oasis free from the stresses of daily life. In reality, it takes work to make *any* house a peaceful home. There needs to be unity of purpose, for children are adept at playing one parent off of the other. When there are two religions vying for primacy, things are usually much worse. It is not uncommon for kids of intermarriage to use religion as a weapon — "Daddy was mean to me so I'm taking off the Star of David he gave me" or "I want him to buy me a bike

so I'll let him see me reading the Easter book he gave me."
In unhealthy situations such as these, it is very unlikely
that the kids will grow up with a positive and healthy attitude towards their Jewish identities.

Furthermore, intermarriage self-help books and therapists are known to warn parents of anger that may be di-
rected at them when the kids are in the teens. Many
children of intermarriage express real and deep anger at
their parents for putting them in such a difficult situation
— for leaving them in the middle of an issue that the parents themselves could not resolve. The kids, even when
they get older, are caught in a terrible bind. Often their in-
ner need to belong pushes them to want to choose one
religious identity, but they fear doing so because uncon-
sciously it feels like they are choosing one parent over another. And the problem goes past subconscious feelings
— in most cases even adult children of intermarriage are
effectively blocked from choosing either religious or ethnic community because of how much they perceive that it
would hurt their parents. Their problems start in childhood but do not end there.

Conclusion

There are indeed some children of intermarriage who
grow up well adjusted and comfortable with their place in
the world. However, they seem to constitute a minority. In
a large number of cases, damage is being done to children
growing up in intermarried homes, no matter the particular arrangement that the parents made with each other or

the particular combination of religions in question. These children lack a clear identity and a true sense of belonging. They miss out on both the practical and psychological advantages of being fully connected to one religious and ethnic community. The latent religious conflict between parents (who would really have preferred to have the kids raised with the same religious background with which they were raised) often hurts the family dynamic as a whole. Kids are put in the middle, complicating the creation of strong bonding and closeness with their parents, thus missing out on what is possibly the single most important ingredient in raising healthy and happy kids: a close-knit, unified family.

Notes

1. Cited in *Modern Man in Search of a Soul* (London: Began, Paul, 1933), 244.
2. Special thanks to Rabbi Charles Lebeau for his help in this section.
3. As we will see in the next section, in almost all cases, even those children of intermarriage who are raised as "Jews only" end up without a clear Jewish identity, for the "other religion" often makes its way into the home despite early agreements.
4. Winer and Meir, *Questions Jewish Parents Ask*, 19.
5. Upon reading this manuscript in September 2002, psychologist and author Dr. Lisa Aiken emphasized to me that while some parents shy away from "imposing" one religion on children because they fear it will harm them, the opposite is actually true! Numerous studies have shown that children need one clear religious identity to be psychologically healthy, as explained above.
6. Petsonk and Remsen, *Intermarriage Handbook*, 194.

7. In fact, the rapid spread of counselors, therapists, workshops, and self-help literature on the subject in itself attests to the growing recognition of the problems associated with intermarriages!

8. Petsonk and Remsen, *Intermarriage Handbook*, 20.

Being Jewish and Staying Jewish

Chapter 4

Mark Twain and Me

As you may have noticed, much of *Why Marry Jewish?* is surprisingly rather un-Jewish. That is to say, it has little to do with the Jewish people or Judaism per se. Until now, we have focused on general principles, studies, and experiences that apply broadly to all intermarriages. We have seen that because of latent religious and cultural feelings and loyalties, sooner or later serious problems are likely to develop. Chances are that it'll be difficult for you, your marriage, and your kids. We haven't focused particularly on a "Jewish" approach, as in theory all of this could apply to any interfaith marriage.[1]

But being Jewish is a unique gift, and the loss of Jewishness from a family is a unique and tragic loss. We should, therefore, at least begin to explore the "Jewish aspects" of the intermarriage question.

Feeling Jewish

Scanning the horizon today, Judaism seems like a relatively small religion: numerically, we are less than 14 million people worldwide by most counts, only a drop in the bucket compared to Christianity, Islam, Buddhism, or many of the other African and Asian religions that exist. However, let us look beyond the numbers. Let us consider the message of Judaism and its impact, including our past and future, as well as our present.

The Jewish people is literally the oldest nation on earth, and have somehow survived generation after generation. King Louis XIV of France once asked the great philosopher Pascal for proof that there is some kind of supernatural force in the world. "Why, the Jews, your majesty," Pascal answered, "the Jews."

I think of this often. My wife and I recently moved to central Israel, a twenty-minute drive south of the Jerusalem-Tel Aviv highway. Several thousand families live in a new town built on a picturesque hilltop. The other hilltops surrounding us remain as ours was only ten years ago — barren, rocky, and empty. That is how most of Israel looked for the last two thousand years, by all historical accounts.

Now things have changed. The country is alive again. Terrorism notwithstanding, the Jewish people's return to our ancient homeland after two thousand years of longing is nothing less than a modern miracle. Yet even before this physical return to the Jewish homeland fully materialized, we were already known to be a people of miracles. In 1899, Mark Twain observed:

If the statistics are right, the Jews constitute but one percent of the human race. It suggests a nebulous dim puff of stardust lost in the blaze of the Milky Way. Properly the Jew ought hardly to be heard of; but he is heard of, has always been heard of. He is as prominent on the planet as any other people, and his commercial importance is extravagantly out of proportion to the smallness of his bulk. His contributions to the world's list of great names in literature, science, art, music, finance, medicine, and abstruse learning are also way out of proportion to the weakness of his numbers. He has made a marvelous fight in this world, in all the ages, and has done it with his hands tied behind him. He could be vain of himself, and be excused for it. The Egyptian, the Babylonian, and the Persian rose, filled the planet with sound and splendor, then faded to dream stuff and passed away; the Greek and the Roman followed, and made a vast noise, and they are gone; other peoples have sprung up and held their torch high for a time, but it burned out, and they sit in twilight now, or have vanished. The Jew saw them all, beat them all, and is now what he always was, exhibiting no decadence, no infirmities of age, no weakening of his parts, no slowing of his energies, no dulling of his alert and aggressive mind. All things are mortal but the Jew; all other forces pass, but he remains. What is the secret of his immortality?[2]

Twain aptly pointed out both Jewish longevity and contributions to the world. In truth, our greatest contribution to the world has been ethical monotheism.[3] Without exception, ancient cultures (including the "great" Greeks and Romans) practiced human sacrifice and killing for entertainment. They commonly murdered babies that had even minor "deformities" such as a harelip, or simply because they wanted a boy instead of a girl. It was the Torah, the Bible, which taught that we human beings are God's children created in the "Divine Image"[4] and that all of us — including men, women, and children — have the right to life and respect. "Thou shalt not murder," the sixth commandment, gave the world its first absolute rule that murder is simply wrong.

In a world that for millennia saw violence and war as glorious, the Jewish prophets taught that while self-defense was necessary, the true ideal was "beating swords into plowshares and spears into pruning hooks."[5] Our vision has become the universal ideal — these words appear on the outside of the United Nations building in New York City.

In a world of elitism, despotism, and slavery, the Torah instructed that "justice, justice you will pursue,"[6] and that we should set up courts of law to protect the oppressed. In a world of ignorance, Jews celebrated and shared knowledge and have always been known as the world's most literate nation.

The Greeks and the Romans, the epitome of ancient civilization, were, as Rabbi Ken Spiro put it, "brilliant in engineering, astronomy, literature, art, science, mathematics, and politics, but these ancient societies did not produce the morality and values we cherish today."[7] Who was it then that civilized and "moralized" the world?

We did.

British historian Paul Johnson explained that it was our ideas and teachings that made the difference:

> Certainly the world without the Jews would have been a radically different place.... To them we owe the idea of equality before the law, both divine and human; of the sanctity of life and the dignity of the human person; of individual conscience and also of personal redemption; of the collective conscience and also of social responsibility; of peace as an abstract ideal and love as the foundation of justice, and many other items which constitute the basic moral furniture of the human mind. Without the Jews the world would have been a much emptier place.... It is almost beyond our capacity to imagine how the world would have fared if they had never emerged.[8]

Without looking into Jewish history and religious thought, one can easily ignore our incredible survival and contribution. But what an impact we have had — and from such a tiny, oppressed people!

In truth, our contribution to the world is not only in the past, but also in the present and future. Even today,

Jews play an essential and disproportionate role in strengthening the world's conscience and helping humanity progress in morality as well as technology. It is not only Jewish people who are very influential in many spheres of modern endeavor, but also Jewish ideas that continue to affect the world.

For this reason, it is no coincidence that the worst elements of society always target the Jews — they know that our continued existence testifies to the truth of the Torah's teachings and the greatness of the human soul. As Hitler put it in his famous quotation: "The Jews have inflicted two wounds on humanity: circumcision on its body and conscience on its soul."[9] For those who want to deny morality and conscience, the disappearance of the Jews is therefore essential. By criticizing, blaming, persecuting, and targeting the Jews, the lowest elements of society promote and justify themselves. Those of us who want to bring true morality and goodness to the entire world, and those who wish to deny Hitler a posthumous victory, are determined to see the Jewish people survive and flourish.

We All Count

Despite the dual threats of anti-Semitism and assimilation, the Jewish people as a whole will survive. We have, as the quotations above showed, survived thousands of years. We are not going to "disappear" now. The great Russian writer Tolstoy understood this reality and wrote:

> The Jew is the emblem of eternity. He whom
> neither slaughter nor torture of thousands
> of years could destroy. He whom neither fire
> nor sword nor inquisition was able to wipe
> off the face of the earth. He who was the first
> to produce the oracles of God. He who has
> been for so long the guardian of prophecy,
> and who transmitted it to the rest of the
> world — such a nation cannot be destroyed.
> The Jew is as everlasting as is eternity itself. [10]

Tolstoy was far from the first to notice our longevity. In fact, in the Bible itself God promises Abraham that the Jewish people will not disappear: "And I will establish My covenant between Me and you and your descendants after you throughout their generations, an eternal covenant, to be your God and the God of the descendants after you." [11]

Nevertheless, important questions remain. To start off with, while we have rebounded tremendously from the Holocaust, we are still far away from what we could be achieving as a people, for ourselves and for the world. We are suffering staggering losses in numbers due to assimilation. What kind of a Jewish people will we have? Small, disorganized, and on the defensive, or healthy, knowledgeable, and proud?

Secondly, what is your role in all this? To approach this question, let me share a story.

I once spent some time with an old friend that I'm

quite fond of. Bright, well-meaning guy. I was already very "into" being Jewish. He wasn't. I gently encouraged him to learn a little about Judaism. "Look," I said, in an attempt to avoid being accused of brainwashing, "you can just come to a class or two, and then go back to your same life. No one is going to starve you, hypnotize you, beat you, threaten you, or force you to stop driving on Saturdays. You'll just get some exposure to the great ideas that have been part of Jewish life for centuries. You've always had so much work pressure that you've never had time to actually learn about all this impressive stuff. No one will push you to do anything, and you'll walk away a little more knowledgeable than before. Besides," I smiled, "I know for a fact that you're not doing anything today anyway!"

I was quite proud of my little monologue, thought that I had carefully managed to explain myself without offending, and put forth an offer that he couldn't refuse. To my surprise, he answered, "I have a right to remain ignorant and you can't push anything on me. It is my life and this is a free country. This ain't Iran, you know."

He got me thinking. Perhaps he was right. Is there such a thing as a "right" to ignorance?

Needless to say, my friend's suggestion wasn't particularly smart. If I could present to you a reasonable argument that there is five hundred dollars waiting for you in your jacket pocket and all you have to do is reach your hand in and get it, it would be foolish of you not to check it out. However, if you don't want to reach into your pocket to find out what is really there, you have a right to do that. It *is* a free country, after all. Despite the fact that Judaism will bring you more happiness than five hundred dollars, you have the right to remain ignorant.

Taking the example a little further, consider the same money-in-the-pocket case if you are starving. The decision not to bother reaching your hand into your pocket is even less comprehensible, but I suppose you could argue the same point. Perhaps then also you would have the right to remain ignorant of the contents of your pocket.

But what if you have a family that depends on you and has no other means of support? What if they really need the money to survive? Would you still have the right not to check in your pocket?

Interdependent World

The truth is that no one lives in a vacuum. Between terrorism, worldwide economic markets, and environmental issues, we are starting to appreciate the idea that the world is interdependent. Our individual actions affect the world around us.

This concept is fundamental to Jewish philosophy and life. The very idea of monotheism, that there is one God, implies this idea. If there are many gods roaming around warring against each other, etc., then some people will be aligned with one god, some with another, and some people may simply fall through the cracks. Once we realize that there is only one God, however, and that He both knows and cares about everyone, nobody falls through the cracks. Everyone counts.

How I live my life matters. I don't simply have the "right" to remain ignorant and do whatever I want. Others depend on me. Whether I want to or not, I act as an example to others around me.

The point is that the Jewish future depends on you. You may not be rich, famous, or even particularly learned, but you are part of an intrinsic whole. You affect other people. If you intermarry, you will make intermarriage more acceptable among those who know you, helping to cause other intermarriages. If you intermarry, you deny another Jew the possibility of finding a Jewish spouse, and weaken the Jewish people as a whole.

Conversely, when you make marrying a Jew a priority in your life, you strengthen the Jewish people religiously, socially, and economically. When you are active on behalf of the Jewish people, you inspire others to do the same. When you marry another Jew, you help ensure that the vitality, creativity, and strength of your children and their children will contribute to the Jewish future.

Consider the following example. Let us say that you have three children and each of your descendants also has three children. That means the first generation of your descendants will number three. The second will number nine. The third generation will number twenty-seven. The fourth will number eighty-one. The fifth will number 243. The sixth will number 729. The seventh will number 2187. The eighth will number 6561. The ninth will number 19,683. The tenth generation will number 59,049

Jews. In only ten generations, that is a lot of people who vote, demonstrate, contribute, live, pray, and are active on behalf of Jews worldwide. And all because of how you made Jewish decisions. Not bad for one person!

Notes

1. Rather than focusing on the "Jewish angle" of what intermarriage is doing to the Jewish people as a whole, this book has focused on issues of personal happiness. This decision was based on my personal experience of what people are interested in hearing about. Already fifty years ago, one of the expert researchers in the field, Judson T. Landis, wrote, "Catholics, Protestants, and Jews have frowned upon mixed marriages and have done much to discourage their young people from entering mixed unions. Some young people feel that the discouraging of mixed unions among the followers of different faiths is largely a battle for the souls and that there is no practical reason why they should not enter mixed marriages. Many young people today are probably not much interested in the struggle for souls, but they are interested in knowing whether a mixed marriage has less chance for success than a marriage within a faith" (Judson T. Landis, "Marriages of Mixed and Non-Mixed Religious Faith," *American Sociological Review* 14 [1949]: 402). In fact, Landis found that there are indeed many practical reasons for not entering into a mixed marriage.

2. From "Concerning the Jews," *Harpers*, 1899; see *The Complete Essays of Mark Twain* (Doubleday, 1963), 249.

3. I am indebted to the research and writing of Rabbi Ken Spiro for the information in this section, especially his essay "World Perfect," which appeared in *Jewish Matters*. His book on the subject, *WorldPerfect*, was released by Simcha Press in September 2002.

4. Genesis 1:27.

5. Isaiah 2:4; Micah 4:3.

6. Deuteronomy 16:20.

7.   Spiro, "World Perfect," in *Jewish Matters*, 24.

8.   Johnson, *History of the Jews*, epilogue.

9.   It is no coincidence that the Greeks, Nazis, and others targeted circumcision, for it represents the fact that we are not born perfect, but rather need to overcome our physical natures rather than give in to them.

10. "What is a Jew?" from *Jewish World* (London, 1908).

11. Genesis 17:7.

Chapter 5

The Jewish Home

What do you think is the center of Jewish life? The synagogue? The Jewish community center? The kosher deli?

The real center of Jewish life is the Jewish home. This may shock you. After all, most Jews today grow up with little explicitly Jewish about their homes. Perhaps they have a mezuzah[1] on the doorpost, a few Jewish books on the shelves, and eat matzoh on Passover. Many Jewish people's homes today aren't even as Jewishly identified as that — their home lives have little particularly Jewish about them at all. Sometimes, people don't think of themselves as having Jewish homes at all — they are Jewish people who have homes, but not necessarily Jewish ones.

Today, the few connections that most Jews have to Judaism are focused on the synagogue. That is where they express themselves Jewishly by attending the High Holiday services. That is where their bar or bat mitzvah took place, and that is where they hope to get married. Their Judaism is synagogue-centered. And there is no doubt that the synagogue serves vital roles in terms of Torah study, community development, and public prayer.

But let us focus on the home. The overwhelming number and high priority of home-based Jewish laws and customs are astounding. The celebration of Shabbat, that beautiful weekly respite to bring meaning and connections into family life, is home-based. Similarly, all the Jewish holidays enable families to retreat from the outside world in order to share some meaningful time together in the fortress they call home. Jewish holidays spent at home with loved ones give kids the love, affection, and sense of belonging that they crave and remember much longer than we realize. The commandment of keeping kosher, which infuses meaning into the physical act of eating, is mostly home-based. Jewish homes are filled with Jewish books, artwork, and have mezuzahs on the doorposts. Many other mitzvot are home-based as well, and Jewish homes are filled with talk of Judaism and contemporary Jewish issues.

Some intermarried Jewish parents feel that even if their home lives will be largely void of Jewishness, at least their non-Jewish spouse agrees to let the kids go to religious school at the synagogue. This will, they hope, "make up" for what is missing in the home. But when the school teaches how important Judaism is, and the underlying message of the home is that Judaism is not important (as witnessed by the fact of the intermarriage itself), the home takes precedence. Hebrew school teachers will not be taken seriously when Judaism is not taken seriously in the home, because the home defines children's true priorities, and parents are children's main role models. Parents with kids in Hebrew school will tell you what their Hebrew school directors tell them — a child's Jewish identity depends on the environment of the home much more than what is taught at school. As much as synagogues and Jewish schools are important to the Jewish people, solid Jewish homes are even more important.

Consider these words from nationally syndicated radio talk show host Dennis Prager:

> Judaism is almost entirely home-based. Any rabbi will tell you that the home is more important religiously than the synagogue. And homes are made by married couples. A Jew cannot lead a fully Jewish life if the people in his or her home are not Jewish.[2]

When people consider the home to be a minor or irrelevant part of Jewish life, the choice of a non-Jewish marriage partner does not seem of particular concern. But when a person realizes that the home is really the single most important factor in forming a child's Jewish identity, then the identities, allegiances, and priorities of the members of that home become crucial.

Rabbi Paysach Freedman of Jerusalem agrees:

> Who you marry affects every single aspect of your life. It affects your community. It affects your children. It affects all future generations. The Jewish home is the single most

important establishment in Jewish life. It outweighs any synagogue or temple, even the Holy Temple built by King Solomon.[3]

As mentioned above, many Jews today have lost much of the Jewishness of their homes. The reasons may relate to the fact that it seems easier to go to synagogue a couple of times a year and be passive than to have to learn "what to do" at home. Also, many people simply lack an example of what a Jewish home can look like. However, no matter the level of Jewish activity, when both parents are Jewish the people growing up in the home usually still feel that they are part of something. While they may not be extremely proactive about being Jewish, they usually know who they are.

What effect does a mixed home have on a child's outlook and sense of priorities? Where the marriage is mixed, Jewishness necessarily becomes less central to home life. After all, one parent doesn't identify with it. When the Jewish spouse wants to incorporate Jewish living, the non-Jewish spouse often feels alienated. Fairness requires that the non-Jewish spouse has his or her input also. As we will see, Jewishness in intermarried families rarely lasts.[4]

With the understanding that the home is the center of Jewish life, and that the Jewishness of the children depends much more on the Jewishness of the home they grow up in than on any other factor, the implications for the choice of a marriage partner should be obvious.

Notes

1. A mezuzah is a small parchment with important Jewish prayers written on it. It is usually enclosed in an attractive cover or box and is hung on doorposts.
2. *Ultimate Issues*, volume 9:2, p. 15.
3. Cited in an Ask-the-Rabbi e-mail from www.ohr.edu on July 23, 2000.
4. See next section, "Will the Kids Stay Jewish?"

Chapter 6

Will the Kids Stay Jewish?

Hopes, dreams, and rationalizations aside, the reality is that children of intermarriage are extremely unlikely to identify as Jews when they mature into adults. This conclusion was predicted by Marshall Sklar, widely known as the foremost sociologist of American Jewry of the twentieth century:

> Many intermarried parents declare...that upon maturity their child will have the right to choose his own identity. This generally means that his identity will be with the majority group...the majority of the children of intermarried Jews, then, will be Gentiles.[1]

As we will see, sadly, Dr. Sklar's prediction has been proven to be correct. The explanation is important:

Hebrew University's researcher Dr. Peter Medding studied what keeps families Jewish generation after generation. He found that the key is giving children what he calls an "unambiguous Jewish identity."[2] This conclusion is not surprising. We live in an overwhelmingly non-Jewish society with powerful media and cultural influences pushing us away from identification with a Jewish minority comprising less than 2% of the general population. If the children involved do not grow up "unambiguously" Jewish, there is little chance of any Jewishness surviving long term. As we will see, intermarriages almost never provide the needed "unambiguous Jewish identity."

The Sad Facts

The obvious question, then, concerns numbers — what actually happens to the children of intermarriage? The results of multiple surveys on the subject have been consistent:

- At most 18% of the children of intermarriage are being raised as "Jewish only."[3] Even this minority celebrate Christmas more than they celebrate Passover![4]

- 65% of children of intermarriage go to church as teens, yet only 19% go to synagogue as teens. Only 14% had a bar or bat mitzvah.[5]

- 62% of the children of intermarriage have a Christmas tree;[6] 81% help decorate a Christmas tree and 93% give and/or receive Christmas presents.[7]

- Only 15% of mixed married families belong to a synagogue and only 16% belong to any other Jewish organization.[8]

- Tellingly, only 18% of the children of intermarriage agree with the statement "being Jewish is very important to me."[9] Only 11% would be "very upset" if their kids did not regard themselves as Jews.[10]

In May, 2001, Professor Sylvia Barack Fishman of Brandeis University released a new study which looked in-depth at American interfaith families and confirmed many people's fears that intermarriage was essentially a stepping-stone out of the Jewish people.

Aside from verifying previous studies of extremely low Jewish identity rates among the children of intermarriage (82% of mixed married households celebrate Christmas in some form; 79% celebrate Christmas despite having an agreement to raise the kids as Jews; 66% celebrate Easter in some form),[11] perhaps the most important point that the study revealed was that the Christian-ness of intermarried homes increases over the years. The study found that whether or not the mother is Jewish, most interfaith families — even those raising their children as Jews — incorporate substantial Christian celebrations into their lives, often including more Christian aspects as the couple and their children age.[12]

> After years of marriage, even in households that initially relegated Christian activities to

the households of extended families, bound-
aries between Christian and Jewish activities
softened, and Jewish spouses agreed to
move Christmas and/or Easter festivities
into their "Jewish" homes, especially as
non-Jewish grandparents aged.[13]

Despite good intentions in the early years, the Jewish
messages intermarried families send get more and more
diluted as the children age. The classic example quoted
from Dr. Barack Fishman's study was the celebration of
Christmas and Easter. Many Jewish parents initially refuse to celebrate these Christian holidays in their home.
However, they "eventually compromise out of a desire to
be fair to their spouses" or because the previous arrangement (i.e., going to the Christian grandparents for those
holidays) gets harder as the years go by and the grandparents get older. As one intermarried Jewish woman put it:

> I love my mother-in-law, and she just can't do it
> any more. So now it's my pleasure to make Easter
> dinner for her and her family. I even make them
> ham, because it means a lot to them.[14]

In fact, as a different study stated, "even some of the
most Jewish of the mixed married couples maintain
Christian observances in the home."[15] Dr. Fishman concluded that, in fact, "the great majority of mixed-married
households incorporate substantial Christian celebrations into their family life."[16]

What Will the Kids Choose?

The most surprising statistics are undoubtedly those concerning the 18% of the children of intermarriages who are being officially raised as "Jews only." They are considered the Jewish "elite" among all the children of intermarriages. Sadly, official family policy notwithstanding, only a handful of them end up being raised as "Jews only." Former agreements can be directly or indirectly changed, based on new realities and old feelings. Furthermore, no matter what parents try to encourage, it is far from guaranteed that the kids will themselves identify as Jews.

Consider the following interchange from a radio talk show in California:

> *A woman calls in: "I'm Jewish," she says. "My husband is not Jewish, but he is very active in the Jewish community. We are trying our best to raise our children as Jews and give them a Jewish education. Now my son is almost thirteen, and he tells us he doesn't want a bar mitzvah. What can we do?"*
>
> *"Let me get this straight," the host says. "You say your husband is not Jewish?"*
>
> *"That's right," the woman answers.*
>
> *"How do you expect your son to follow Judaism when you don't?"*

Actions speak louder than words. If being Jewish was really that important, children subconsciously sense, then Mommy wouldn't have married out. By marrying out she has demonstrated that Judaism is of little relevance. Why should the kids then listen to exhortations about the importance of being Jewish?

Similarly, one adolescent raised with the dual-religion approach remarked, "It was your idea that I should be both Christian and Jewish. But I'm not a little kid anymore and I believe in Jesus. It is *my* life."

Most of the Jewish parents involved, if asked during their engagement period, would certainly have answered that "yes, our kids will identify as Jews." But the reality is otherwise. Intermarriage does not — indeed almost cannot — provide the "unambiguous Jewish identity" that is needed to keep Jewishness alive in the family.[17] After all, as long as one spouse is not Jewish, "it is hard to exclude Christian rituals, ceremonies, and culture from family life."[18]

Children of Intermarriage Intermarry

With their remarkably low levels of Jewish identification, it is not surprising that while about 59% of the children of in-married families say marrying a Jewish person is highly important to them, only 13% of those from mixed-married families consider marrying another Jew to be "very" or "extremely" important![19] In fact, the "adult children of mixed marriages are overwhelmingly mixed married themselves."[20] Studies have confirmed the sad reality that over 90% of the children of intermarriage themselves marry non-Jews.[21] Also, 97% of them have no plans to "discourage" their children "from marrying someone who is not Jewish."[22] The Jewish link is thus lost forever.

Lost Jews

Basing himself on the numbers from the 1990 National Jewish Population Survey, Daniel J. Elazar took a different approach in studying the effects of intermarriage.[23] He calculated the number of Jews "lost" to assimilation:

> The survey found that there were 590,000 people who were born or raised as Jews who now are either nothing or have another religion. About 210,000 of these told the interviewers that they had converted to another religion. The other 380,000 of Jewish parentage or background with another religion may be examples of Milton Himmelfarb's famous dictum, which he posed as a question: "What do you call the grandchildren of intermarried Jews?" His answer: "Christians."

Other commentators have used a similar approach: after the Holocaust, there were 12 million Jews. Now there are 13 million. By any standard measure of population growth, we should now, at least, be back to our pre-war size of 18 million. The truth is that while some Jews may have openly converted to other religions, the vast majority simply faded away through intermarriage and assimilation.

Many people feel that they can "have their cake and eat it too" — that is to say, intermarry and still raise Jewish children. As we have seen, the reality is that in all likelihood, when a Jew marries a non-Jew, his or her Jewish legacy will be lost forever no matter what particular strategies the family adopts in order to keep the kids Jewish.

The statistical evidence in study after study is clear and convincing: it is extremely unlikely that one can intermarry and raise children with a clear Jewish identity. Only a small minority of the children of intermarriage will consider themselves to be Jews. Only a miniscule percentage will marry Jews and encourage their children to identify and marry Jewishly. As one report put it, "despite the hopes and assumptions, Jewish identification does not fare well in mixed marriages.... The likelihood of creating an unambiguous Jewish identity...is virtually nil."[24]

Whether it happens to the children or grandchildren of the couple in question,[25] intermarriage almost inevitably leads to the complete loss of a family's Jewish heritage.

Notes

1. Sklar, *America's Jews*, 202.
2. Medding, et al. *Jewish Identity*, 37–38.
3. Of the rest, 33% are being raised Christian only, 24% in "no religion" homes, and 25% in "dual religion" homes. (Phillips, *Re-examining Intermarriage*, 49, fig. 2–3. This study is based primarily on the intermarriage data taken from the 1991 National Jewish Population Survey, as well as follow-up research done in 1993.)
4. Ibid., table 2-5, p. 52. Those who are being raised as "Jews only" in homes with one Jewish parent and one non-religious

parent score 2.6 out of 3 for Christmas observances and only 1.8 out of 3 for Passover observances. Those who are being raised as "Jews only" in homes with one Jewish parent and one openly Christian parent score 2.5 out of 3 for Christmas observances and only 1.5 out of three for Passover observances. Despite these disheartening numbers, these "Jews only" children are the Jewish "cream of the crop" when it comes to the products of intermarriages. In other constellations, whether the children are being raised as "no religion" or Christian, Christmas observances remain as high or higher and Passover observances are almost non-existent.

5.   Mayer, *Children of Intermarriage*. Some other statistics: 83% of the children of intermarriage perceived "no greater responsibility to fellow Jews than [to] others in need"; 70% felt they had no greater responsibility to support Israel than other Americans, or at all; 81% deemed "unimportant" the act of belonging to the Jewish community. Only 9% felt studying about Judaism was very important.

6.   Medding et al., *Jewish Identity*, table 29, p. 67. Compare this with only 2% of in-married families that have a Christmas tree. The authors note that the degree of Christian observances and identification are essential in defining Jewish identity: "Our theory of Jewish identity posited that being not Christian was a major defining element of Jewish identity. The creation of an unambiguous Jewish identity entails, at the very least, the absence from the home of Christian symbols and practices, even if the level of Jewish identification is low."

7.   Mayer, *Children of Intermarriage*.

8.   Compared to 60% and 57% respectively of in-married families. Medding et al., *Jewish Identity*, table 18, p. 53 and table 21, p. 58.

9.   Mayer, *Children of Intermarriage*. Additionally 59% flatly disagreed, and 23% were uncertain. Similarly, the Jewish Community Center's Maccabi Teen Survey of May 1994 found that "children of interfaith families have significantly lower levels of Jewish identity than do children in in-married or conversionary families." (Sales, *Values and Concerns*, 23.

See also p. 28.)

10.   Ibid., 18% were uncertain, 71% would not be upset.

11.   Fishman, "Jewish and Something Else," 45.

12.   Ibid., 8. Dr. Fishman deliberately over-represented the per-
       centage of intermarried families who were at least attempting
       to raise their children as Jewish, and yet writes that the "per-
       sistent and recurring influence of Christianity even in mixed-
       married families who consider themselves to be raising their
       children as Jews [is] all the more striking" (p. 41).

13.   Ibid., 8.

14.   Ibid., 47.

15.   Phillips, Re-examining Intermarriage, 72.

16.   Fishman, "Jewish and Something Else," 45.

17.   As in this entire volume, please remember that a sincere con-
       vert is a full Jew and a marriage between a born-Jew and a sin-
       cerely converted Jew is not an intermarriage at all, but rather
       a marriage of two Jews.

18.   Fishman, "Jewish and Something Else," 81.

19.   Sales, Values and Concerns, 23.

20.   Fishman, "Jewish and Something Else," 7.

21.   1990 Council of Jewish Federations' National Jewish Popula-
       tion Survey data. Dr. Steven Bayme, "Intermarriage and
       American Jewry: Communal Policy and Program Direction" in
       Intermarriage: What Can We Do? What Should We Do?, 3. See
       also Winer and Meir, Questions Jewish Parents Ask, p. 1 and p.
       19 for more on this.

22.   Mayer, Children of Intermarriage: 6% were uncertain, 91%
       would not discourage their children.

23.   In the Jerusalem Letter published by the Jerusalem Center for
       Public Affairs (vol. 118, Jan. 1991).

24.   Medding et al., Jewish Identity, 37.

25.   As we've seen, the chances of the children of intermarriage
       identifying as Jews are very small. Those few who do identify
       as Jews have such weak Jewish identities and marry non-Jews
       at such high rates (over 90%), that the chances of their chil-
       dren (the grandchildren of intermarriage) identifying as Jews
       are almost non-existent. In fact, a 1984 study by the Jewish
       Federation of Philadelphia could not find one grandchild of in-

termarriage who identified him or herself as Jewish (quoted in Bayme, "Intermarriage and American Jewry," 6). In sum, while sometimes there is a delayed reaction of a generation or two, intermarriage effectively ends Jewishness in a family.

Chapter 7

The Day After

Jews who intermarry often feel that they won't have any problems if they get their non-Jewish spouses to agree to raise the kids as Jews. In this way, they feel, despite intermarrying, their kids will indeed be Jewish and their family's Jewish legacy will continue. The reality is quite different from this rosy picture, as we've discussed.

Furthermore, unfortunately, we live in a world where divorce has become the rule rather than the exception. People today get married hoping that they won't get divorced, but knowing that it might happen. As we saw,[1] intermarriages are even more likely to end in divorce than same-religion marriages.

Before getting intermarried, therefore, it is prudent to think through the implications of divorce on the Jewishness of the children:

> Whether or not you agree to raise your children Jewish is not of much relevance. If for some reason the marriage doesn't work out,

all agreements are void. This happened to someone I know. They agreed to raise their daughter Jewish and have a Jewish home. After the couple's second anniversary, they filed for divorce. Within a year of their separation, the daughter was telling her Jewish father about her religious school classes at church.[2]

Sadly, stories like these are not uncommon. Consider the following newspaper report:

Jeffrey Kendall wanted his children to believe their Jewish mother was destined to burn in hell. The children, attending their father's fundamentalist Christian church, were told that [they] would be doomed if they did not accept Jesus as their lord and savior. It was not always this way for the Kendall family. Kendall and Barbara Zeitler were married in a Jewish ceremony in 1988. Kendall was nominally a Catholic and Zeitler was a mildly observant Reform Jew. They agreed to raise their children, now ages four, six, and nine, as Jews.... By some estimates, one out of three American Jews now lives in an interfaith household.... During the past two decades, a growing number of children have been placed in situations in which one of the parents has sought to change the religious identification of the child over the objections of the other. There have been cases...in which a child, a year before bar mitzvah, was told by the custodial parent that they would no longer be Jewish and henceforth would be a member of another religion..... In other instances, parents like Kendall have actively sought to discredit their children's religious upbringing and convert them to another religion.[3]

People in love don't like to think about divorce. But with divorce rates as high as they are, and the chances of divorce even higher in intermarriages, it is important to acknowledge that the reality of "the day after" needs to be considered. With divorce, all previous agreements are null and void.

Notes

1.   See chapter entitled "Happily Ever After."
2.   Silverman, *Staying Jewish*, 21. Note that similar concerns exist in unfortunate cases where one or both parents die, i.e., Who will get custody? What religious instruction will the kids receive?
3.   Jewish Telegraphic Agency national lead story, "Kids of Intermarriage Get Caught in Crossfire of Divorce," December 19, 1997. Carried in newspapers around the world.

Chapter 8

Are We Racist?

Consider the following:

> When I spoke recently to a group of Jewish college students...I asked for a show of hands as to how many preferred to marry a fellow Jew. The students looked at each other awkwardly and about half the hands went up. I then asked those who had raised their hands how many would be prepared to tell their dorm-mates of their preference. A small number of hands were raised. In the language of the day, it is "politically incorrect" to insist on marrying a co-religionist."[1]

As the author of the quotation, Alan Dershowitz, professor of law at Harvard University, makes abundantly clear, many Jews today would indeed like to marry other Jews, but are made to feel "narrow-minded" or "racist" if they oppose intermarriage. One recent survey found that half of the American Jewish community believes that "it is in fact 'racist' to oppose intermarriages."[2] After all, do we Jews think that we are better than other people? Others phrase the question differently: How can we on the one hand protest anti-Semitism and yet on the other hand refuse to let our kids date non-Jews? Maybe we *are* being narrow-minded.

Let us take a parallel example into consideration:

> *One of the few African-Americans in the office stated in casual conversation that he only wants to date other African-Americans, explaining that while he respects all traditions and peoples, he wants to be involved with someone who can fully share his culture and values. He is being openly criticized by some liberal colleagues for being anti-white. "Whites have come a long way and are willing to go out with you," they say. "Why won't you go out with whites?"*

Who is really being racist — the African-American worker who doesn't want to intermarry or his detractors? In order to properly answer the question, let us think about what racism is — and what it is not.

What Is Universalism?

The open-minded, tolerant ethic on which Western democratic society is based is a vast improvement over other systems that man has developed over the millennia. Throughout most of history, those who were different from the majority culture were stereotyped, oppressed, and often prevented from living the way they wanted to live. Put simply, history has not been kind to minorities.

Today's world has changed significantly from previous centuries. Western culture now espouses respect for different cultures, religions, and ways of life. The Western universalistic ideal focuses on tolerance and multiculturalism. This ideal is basic to our self-definition as modern people. Those who are not universalistic — those who look down on other peoples or cultures — are considered backwards, prejudiced, and just plain wrong.

Yet what exactly is universalism? In our quest to avoid judging other people, how far do we go? Are we forbidden to make any distinctions between groups? If religious and ethnic backgrounds are illegitimate factors in choosing life partners — if people must choose partners based solely on their personalities without any regard to their backgrounds — then statistically speaking individuals from smaller groups will inevitably marry into the "larger culture" at extremely high rates. Immigrant subcultures, for instance, will marry into the majority and disappear within a generation or two after their arrival in America.

That doesn't sound particularly universalistic, does it? If universalism indeed demands that smaller groups effectively give up their identities, then it actually fosters homogeneity rather than respect.

In reality, true universalism lives very well alongside many self-sustaining subcultures. In fact, it requires many different groups of people, not their extinction. After all, if everyone is the same, there isn't much to be universalistic about! Universalism and open-mindedness require respect for other groups. They don't require everyone to be the same, because a society that encourages conformity to one unique religion or culture cannot truly consider itself universalistic. And honest respect for smaller groups and different ways of life requires letting them survive and flourish beyond one generation, which includes respecting their need to encourage "marrying within the group" in order to survive.

With a proper understanding of universalism, we can now return to the example cited above. The African-American in the office was not being racist in wanting to date other African-Americans. Racism does not refer to distinguishing *among* peoples, since we have many interesting and wonderful differences. Racism refers to discriminating *against* people because of their backgrounds. The African-American cited above wasn't stating anything negative about white people at all; he simply wanted to marry someone who fully shared his beliefs, values, and traditions. And his pride in his heritage inspired him to be part of its continuation rather than its termination.

Needed: A New Jewish Attitude

Jews who want to marry Jewish but are embarrassed to say so openly should think along the same lines as this African-American. He earns our respect for attempting to hang on to his heritage. We do not think of him as racist for wanting to spend his life with another African-American. In fact we can easily understand why he wants to marry someone who shares his background, interests, and goals. It is in the interests of his marriage, his children, and his culture.

We Jews should feel the same pride in our three-thousand-year-old heritage, which introduced the ideas of monotheism, kindness, and basic morality into the world. We should want our tradition to be a part of our lives, and want to marry someone who fully identifies with it. We should refer to the following monologue when we need to explain the importance of marrying another Jew.

> *While I may not be the most religious person around, Jewishness is part of me. I want to marry someone that I can fully share it with — someone born Jewish or who sincerely converted. It is not racist to want to be able to share a religion with my spouse — it is good marital planning, and better for the kids to have one clear identity. I also feel part of an incredible history, an incredible tradition that has been passed down for thousands of years. I want my kids to be part of that, and I know that the best way of ensuring a Jewish self-identity is by having two Jewish parents. It is not racist to want to survive — it is noble.*

Notes

1. Dershowitz, *Vanishing American Jew*, 28.
2. Results printed in the *Baltimore Jewish Times* on June 15, 2001 and elsewhere.

Dating

Chapter 9

Not Getting Married?

Much of my early experience as an educator was spent on buses. I was hired to teach and inspire American Jewish youth about Judaism and Israel. It was rewarding work. The organization I worked for had wisely incorporated the principles of "informal education," which believes that out-of-classroom (informal) education is often even more important than in-classroom (formal) education. One explanation for this is very simple: in a formal setting, people feel on the defensive. They put up barriers. When the atmosphere is more relaxed — such as on trips — people open up to new ideas and share their real thoughts.

It was in this atmosphere that I spent weeks and months teaching my fellow Jews. The group members opened up. They were honest and questioning. I felt that I was making a difference.

Based on the work of others before me, I used historic and religious sites to broach topics that were important for them to deal with in their lives as Jews. This chapter deals with a subject that was one of the most important ones for the young people on the bus, and for all single Jews everywhere.

In the North of Israel there is a beautiful site called Tzippori. It is atop a mountain with a magnificent view of the area. Two thousand years ago, Tzippori was an important regional center. Many of the great Jewish sages lived there alongside the "common folk." Many non-Jewish people lived there, too. There are ruins of mosaics, some with Jewish themes and some with decidedly un-Jewish themes. One mosaic that I remember vividly has elegant Jewish symbolism such as pomegranates, one of the seven species of fruit of the Land of Israel. Only a short walk away is a decidedly un-Jewish mosaic featuring the Greek god of alcohol and debauchery, Bachus. The contrast between the two is startling.

In this picturesque setting full of contrasts, the group would discuss the themes of assimilation and intermarriage. How does one maintain one's Jewish culture and religion when surrounded by non-Jewish people and influences? What are "red lines" which cannot be crossed and what are "green lines" in which we can perhaps show more flexibility? What works and what doesn't? How does one measure success and failure?

In our discussions, the topic of intermarriage invariably came up quite quickly. I asked participants how many intended on only marrying another Jewish person. Year after year, about a half of the group raised its hands.

Then I asked another question: how many intend on

only dating other Jews? The highest affirmative response I ever received was 10%. Try this amongst your single Jewish friends, coworkers, etc., and see what the results are. I think your experiences will parallel mine: even among those Jews who want to marry Jewish, few avoid dating non-Jews.

The implications should be considered carefully.

Emotions Are Stronger than You Think

In traditional Jewish life, dating and marriage go "hand in hand." You date because you want to find your life mate. Someone who wants to marry Jewish wouldn't date non-Jews if their main purpose in dating was to find a life partner.

But most Jews today don't date to find their life partners, especially when they are in their teens or early twenties. People date because they like feeling in love. Because it is fun to have a boyfriend (or a girlfriend). Because everyone else is doing it. Because they don't like being alone. But they aren't dating to get married. They feel too young to make decisions like that. They want to gather experiences, to be able to compare and contrast, to "get it out of their system."

According to this modern way of thinking, dating and marriage seem quite disconnected, at least in the early years. It then seems quite reasonable to date non-Jews while still planning to marry Jewish in the end. This is referred to as the "it's just a date" approach. "I'll probably go out with many different people before I settle down," the person tells him or herself. "I have no intention of marrying this person. When I'm ready to get married, I'll look for someone Jewish."

Time and time again, however, the "it's just a date" approach has proven itself to be shortsighted. What I will call "interdating" (Jews dating non-Jews) leads to intermarriage in two ways. First, as you may have guessed, you may end up marrying the person you are "just dating" at the present time.

Consider the following statements:

> "For the first six months I enjoyed going out with her, but had no serious intentions of getting involved…"

> "I had been going with gentile girls before, and I was aware that it could happen [marriage]. But I felt that I would not let it happen to me…."

> "I didn't think it would become serious. At the time I was just going out and enjoying myself."

> "We just drifted together…. One day I just found myself trapped."

The quotes you just read are from real people, recounted in John Mayer's book *Jewish-Gentile Courtships*. It was published in 1961, but the quotes could be from any time or place. They have been repeated many thousands of times in the last few decades. Simply put, we never know what will happen with a relationship. What can start out as an innocent summer romance might last

much longer than expected and turn into a lifelong commitment. Consider the following:

> I was brought up in pretty traditional home. We
> lit candles before sunset on Friday, went to syna-
> gogue on the High Holidays, and were very fo-
> cused on Israel. My parents always said that they
> wanted us to marry Jews, because "marriage is
> hard enough without bringing in different reli-
> gions," as they put it. But they didn't object to my
> dating non-Jewish boys, basically because there
> were very few Jews where we lived and virtually
> none in my high school — how could they forbid
> me to date non-Jews? At college it was the same
> thing — few Jews. No Hillel House, no Chabad.
> The guys I dated were all non-Jewish. Still, I told
> myself that I wanted to marry a Jewish guy. Even
> when Tony and I started going out in senior year,
> I never thought it would last — I mean I was in
> college! But I fell more and more in love and the
> relationship got deeper and deeper. It somehow
> survived three cities and three jobs. I once tried to
> break it off, but I couldn't. I loved him too much
> and cried for the entire month that we weren't to-
> gether. I had my parents broach the subject of
> conversion, because I was too afraid to ask my-
> self. He wasn't at all interested. Nothing to talk
> about. I couldn't bear to be without him, so we
> got married. It was too late — I let myself date

and fall in love with a guy who wasn't Jewish.

As the author of the above piece explained, you never know when a serious relationship will develop, and it gets harder and harder to break off a relationship as time goes by. Feelings grow. External, logical considerations, such as the religion of the person in question, pale compared to the warm feelings of love and romance.

In summary, the first reason that dating non-Jews is problematic is simply because, all too often, casually dating someone allows deep, real feelings to develop.[1] Intermarriage then becomes very likely.

It's All in the Attitude

In order to understand the second problematic aspect of dating non-Jews, let us shift our focus for a moment to the act of giving *tzedakah* (charity). When discussing personality refinement, the great medieval Jewish sage known as Maimonides explained that it is better to give one dollar one hundred times than to give one hundred dollars all at one time. At first glance, this idea is surprising. After all, the same amount of money is being given. The explanation forms the basis for much of Jewish religious thought: external actions affect us internally. By giving charity one hundred times, we will slowly become more generous people. Giving once, even a lot of money, will not have the same effect.

I once tested this principle. I kept a lot of small change on me, and for one month whoever asked was given at least a small coin. At the beginning of the month, I felt quite proud of myself. Within a couple of weeks, it became normal — "Of course I'll try and help someone out," I thought to myself, "anyone would." Then I spent the next month without giving a dime, no matter how pathetic and needy the person was. At first I felt guilty. Those feelings didn't last too long. By the end of the month, I resented every beggar I saw. "Why don't they get a job? Why should my money go to them?" I thought to myself.

What a radical change in attitude! By doing something on a regular basis, it becomes part of you. If you neglect it, it becomes less and less a part of you.

The second major problem of interdating is connected to this principle. It has to do with attitudes. Let us assume for the sake of argument that you really won't marry the person you are dating now. If you want to marry Jewish, dating non-Jews is still a bad idea because the more you date non-Jews, the more the idea of intermarriage seems less problematic. According to Maimonides' principle, actions gradually affect feelings and attitudes; over the long term, priorities change. If you interdate, you become more and more likely to intermarry.

Already in the 1971 National Jewish Population Survey, researchers discovered the important but often overlooked statistic that Jews who intermarried were about four times more likely to have dated non-Jews during their late adolescent years than were those who did not intermarry. While some of the people involved may have actually married their non-Jewish teenage sweethearts, it is reasonable to assume that most did not. Most simply fell into patterns of dating. One important study on inter-marriage concluded the following:

> It is not clear from this study why the ado-lescent patterns are so important, but this finding is consistent with studies of other adolescent behaviors which continue into adulthood. Adults who smoke, for example, begin as teens. Adult criminals usually begin their careers when they are teens. A parallel exists with Jewish mixed marriage. Jews who dated non-Jews in high school married non-Jews as adults.[2]

Let us consider an example of how this change in atti-tudes can work. Consider a college freshman from New York named Adam, with relatively strong Jewish feelings. He is 90% convinced that he is going to marry Jewish, but continues dating non-Jews in the meantime. Although he accepts and identifies with the arguments he's heard against intermarriage (better for the couple, better for the kids, better for the Jewish people), he may want to "broaden his horizons" with non-Jews before settling down with a Jewish spouse. Alternatively, he may indeed want to date Jews, but the practical obstacles to doing this may indeed seem insurmountable — there aren't many Jews on Adam's college campus. It is hard to blame him for thinking that it probably won't do any harm — after all, he doesn't plan on getting married for a decade or more.

But four years of interdating and deepening relationships will inevitably change his perspectives, and his 90% marrying-Jewish conviction may only be 50% by senior year. Why? At this point in Adam's life the most profound relationships he has had have been with non-Jews. His models for relationships are non-Jewish models. He's never had any religious problems with his non-Jewish partners. Even Adam's taste in members of the opposite sex has been subtly changed: non-Jewish habits and a non-Jewish look, if they exist, seem normal to him now, not any less familiar than those of people from the Jewish community that Adam comes from. He doesn't even remember being convinced that marrying Jewish is so important. Still, it would be easier to marry Jewish and he would prefer doing so, all other things being equal.

When Adam gets a job in a city with few single Jews, his marry-Jewish conviction drops even lower. He spends two more years getting more and more comfortable with colleagues' Christmas and Easter celebrations. His Jewish education, identity, and feelings recede further and further into the background. Office romance has bloomed on more than one occasion, and he finds that there is little that he doesn't have in common with the attractive person in question. By the time he is ready to get married, marrying Jewish seems unrealistic and unnecessary. He intermarries.

The more people date non-Jews, the more likely they are to marry out, no matter their "good intentions" when they started out. This is true because even if they don't marry the person they are dating now, their own attitudes, convictions, and priorities change with time. The idea of marrying a non-Jew becomes more and more acceptable at both a conscious and subconscious level, and what seemed highly problematic ten years ago seems perfectly normal now.

Notes

1. On reading this manuscript, psychologist and author Dr. Lisa Aiken mentioned that sometimes precisely because people think that nothing can happen when they are dating a non-Jew, they "let down their defenses," become vulnerable, and fall in love. When this happens, the very assumption that "this won't go anywhere" itself promotes intermarriage!

2. Phillips, *Re-examining Intermarriage*, 39. Two charts (pp. 37, 38) in that same study report on the expectations of adult children of two Jewish parents. When they were in high school, 51% had expected to marry a Jew. But by the time they reached college, only 27% felt that it was "very important" to marry another Jew.

Chapter 10

Love *and* Religion

When all is said and done, how can anyone tell you whom to marry? Don't you have the right to be in love?

Yes, you should have love. And yes, you should be happy. Love is wonderful. Judaism wants you to be in love. God loves love.

How do we know this? The Torah (Bible) itself constantly speaks of love and of how close a husband and wife should feel to each other: "A man shall leave his father and his mother and cling to his wife and they shall become one flesh."[1] Of Isaac and Rebecca the Torah tells us, "...and he loved her."[2] Of Jacob and Rachel, we are told, "Jacob loved Rachel"[3] and worked for fourteen years in order to be able to marry her.

In one of its many statements regarding the love that should exist between a husband and wife, the Talmud teaches that a husband should "love his wife like his own body and honor her even more."[4] Rabbis throughout the ages have even written practical advice on how to improve marriages and create a warm, loving environment in the home.[5] The idea that there should be strong love between husband and wife is fundamental to our entire tradition.

Now that we know how important love is from a Jewish perspective, let us get back to our main question: How can one be asked to sacrifice love in order to "do the right thing?" Sounds callous. And it seems to promise a boring and loveless marriage, which clearly contradicts the Jewish marriage ideal as expressed above.

But If You Love Someone...

You deserve a loving marriage. And you should marry Jewish. These two things are actually perfectly compatible. Consider the following real interview:

> *An American college student is being interviewed. He is wearing a backwards baseball cap and an earring. You get the feeling right away that he is an intelligent and pleasant guy. He is proud of his Jewishness. He mentions how even if his wife is not Jewish, his kids will "definitely be." The interviewer asks him to play out some scenarios. What if she wants a Christmas tree in the house? He hadn't thought of that one, but if it is important to her, he'll agree to it. "Not with Jesus on the cross," he jokes. "A secular one...like a pine tree...with some of those balls on it." Later he is asked about having a priest at the wedding. He*

feels very uncomfortable. What about if she
wants to have the baby baptized? He literally
twists and turns in his seat. Viewers can feel his
struggle. Baptism is the ultimate declaration of al-
legiance to Christianity, and he knows that
throughout Jewish history hundreds of thousands
of our ancestors have died rather than allow
themselves or their children to be baptized. It
seems he is willing to give in. "Look, I don't really
want any of those things. Don't want the Christ-
mas tree. Don't want the priest at the wedding, or
the baptism." He then rhetorically repeats the
question that he is asked by the interviewer, "Why
would I put myself in that position? I don't want
to put myself in that position," he confides, "but if
you love someone...."[6]

This scenario is played out daily across America and
around the world. Many Jews believe that they need to
choose between having love and marrying another Jewish
person. Many, like the personable college student in the
interview described above, realize that they are seriously
compromising their heritage by intermarrying but feel
that there is nothing that can be done about it.

Yet the college student answered his own question.
We can avoid getting into "that position" in the first
place. With a little bit of planning, we can indeed set the
stage so that when that special person comes along, he or
she will be Jewish. Since we can have both love and reli-

gion, we lose nothing and gain everything by marrying another Jew. What people sometimes think must be an either-or situation (i.e., either love *or* religion) simply does not have to end up that way. We can indeed have both love *and* religion.

False Dilemma

Let us step away from intermarriage for a moment in order to put the "love or religion" question into context. In college, my sociology and logic professors often referred to what is called a "false dilemma." A false dilemma is an incorrect use of the word "or" — i.e., this "or" that. A limited number of choices (usually two) is given, while in reality there are more options. One example often used is the struggle between economic development and protecting the environment. Many people and governments feel they must choose between them. But we have learned over the last thirty years that with careful planning and creative thinking, there are ways to develop the economy and protect the environment. The choice of development or the environment is often a false dilemma, because we can usually have both.

The classic question of love or religion is a false dilemma. People think they must choose between them, but really they can have both. Marriages between two Jewish people are just as loving and beautiful as marriages between a Jew and non-Jew — and usually much more so, as illustrated by statistics showing less divorce and greater marital happiness when two Jews marry.[7]

Have Your Cake and Eat It Too

Why does the love or religion question pop up at all? Because people get involved with non-Jews and let their feelings develop. They get to the point that emotionally it simply seems too hard to back out, and they find themselves caught in a difficult position. They are deeply in love with a person who has no Jewish identity. And once you're in love, it is hard to break it off. It certainly seems like a dilemma — love or religion. However, the easiest solution to the dilemma is to avoid the situation in the first place. While there are numerous benefits from friendships with people from various backgrounds, romance should be kept separate. By meeting and dating Jewish people, you can help ensure that the person you fall in love with and marry will be Jewish.[8]

To summarize, the whole love or religion question only arises when someone is already in love with a non-Jew. But you can be just as in love and just as happy with a Jewish person. With a little planning and foresight, you can arrange to have both love and religion.

Notes

1. Genesis 2:24.
2. Ibid. 24:67.
3. Ibid. 29:18.
4. Babylonian Talmud, tractate *Yevamos* 62b.
5. Nachmanides' *Igeres HaKodesh* is one famous example from medieval Europe.
6. Taken from an early version of the *Love & Legacy Seminar* film.

7.   See chapter entitled "Happily Ever After" for statistics.
8.   See following chapter, entitled "Getting Practical," for help in this area.

Chapter 11

Getting Practical

The funny thing about the high intermarriage rates prevalent today is that even though they cannot really explain it, most Jews would indeed prefer to marry other Jews. Somehow they sense that by marrying out they risk losing an important part of themselves. But, as they often explain, though "it would be nice to marry Jewish, one has to deal with reality." Many single Jews today feel that it is simply too difficult to meet another Jewish person with whom they could happily settle down.

To honestly deal with the contemporary intermarriage problem, we need to squarely deal with the practical side: Why do Jews today have difficulty meeting other Jews?

Consider the situation only fifty years ago. Social circles then were largely ethnic and religious. Generally speaking, Catholics socialized with and married other Catholics. Protestants socialized with and married other Protestants. Jews socialized with and married other Jews.

People grew up in one neighborhood, knew everyone in it, and often formed their lifelong friendships during their early years spent there. Even when rising salaries permitted moving into nicer neighborhoods, they usually moved in groups, keeping the same social circles they had had for most of their lives.

Today, fewer and fewer Jews grow up in "Jewish neighborhoods" or socialize with other Jews. The result is that Jews simply don't know as many Jews as they used to. It isn't easy to marry Jewish if you don't know any Jews.

Also, people today rarely meet their mates in their early years anyway. They meet through work. They meet at college. They meet on vacation, at friends' parties, or in a bar. Whatever specific social arena you think of, the reality is that most of the places where eligible singles meet have only a small percentage of Jews. What are the chances that singles will "accidentally" meet other Jews? With the low percentage of Jews in the general population[1] and the low levels of Jewish involvement today, it is a wonder that the intermarriage rates are not even higher!

Essentially, the problem is that dating today is much less often planned or thought out than it used to be. Randomly meeting people in a society whose huge majority is non-Jewish will necessarily lead to high intermarriage rates. In today's world, a person who wants to marry Jewish needs to put some planning into it.

To help you along this all-important path, let's get practical: How should you go about meeting other Jews? Here are some ideas that work.

Go where Jews go.

Today many people meet their mates in informal settings such as the office.[2] The gym. The coffee shop. The li-
brary. The park. The cruise. Often the places where you
make friends are the same places you may meet people
that you'd want to date. If you want to meet more Jews,
go to places where Jews go. Get involved in activities that
other single Jews are involved in. Join a Torah class that
has single Jews your age. Go to the Jewish bakery and
kosher food store. Join the local Jewish community center
and a synagogue that has other single members. Get involved in synagogue life.

Move to a Jewish neighborhood.

In order to make meeting Jews easier, consider moving to a more "Jewish" part of town. In every city today
with a major Jewish population, there are Jewish neighborhoods. While these neighborhoods are not all Jewish,
they have high enough percentages of Jews that forming
Jewish social circles is much easier. We'd all consider
moving to get a good job or a good education — why not
do the same to help ensure that you can find your
soulmate?

Get set up.

In traditional communities past and present, it is relatively easy to meet other Jews. When a person has
reached the age and maturity that they are ready to date,

a third party (often a "*shadchan*," or matchmaker) makes the introduction and the individuals concerned spend the necessary time to see if they think and feel that this is indeed the right person. Sometimes a couple hits it off right away and sometimes people date for years before finding the right person, but the system works well. Why? Because time and emotions are not wasted on people who you'd never want to marry anyway. Your physical and mental energy is reserved for the type of person who you've already decided is in the ballpark before going out.

Think of it like this: just like a board of directors puts thought into what type of person it wants to hire as the next CEO, so too we should spend some time thinking about what kind of person to meet. Just like the board of directors goes to a headhunter to find the right person, so too we should carefully consider how we can meet the right person to spend our lives with.

"Matchmakers" still exist in every city where there is a Jewish community, serving Jews of all stripes, colors, and persuasions.[3] He or she can get to know you and get a sense of who you are and what you are looking for. Sounds archaic at first, I know, but think about it. Here is a person who has met many Jews who also want to meet the right person, and is usually in contact with others who know even more Jewish singles. *No one will tell you who to marry. They will simply help set you up on blind dates.*

Also, note that many of our parents and friends have met through blind dates, and almost everyone has been on some. People want to help. Ask your family and friends to be on the lookout for you — those who know you best can provide some of your best leads.

Good Luck!

Notes

1. Jews comprise less than 2% of the population of the United States, and even less in most other Western countries.
2. Interested readers are referred to Phillips, *Re-examining Inter-marriage*, p. 39, table 1–20, for a fascinating look at where in-marrieds and intermarrieds meet their spouses. In-marrieds were five times more likely to have met their spouses through a blind date than intermarrieds (10% vs. 2%), and about four times less likely to have met their spouses at work (7% vs. 25%). These figures indicate how important it is to carefully consider what types of settings and methods are used to meet members of the opposite sex, for they have a major impact on the likelihood of intermarriage.
3. Internet dating services have become quite popular of late. While they may be of help to certain people, no studies have been done yet as to their effectiveness.

Chapter 12

Final Thoughts

In our modern, multicultural world, arguments against intermarriage may at first seem hopelessly outdated. Yet we should consider the practical side of what is likely to lead to greater marital happiness, less divorce, stronger children, and keeping the kids Jewish. We have seen that intermarriages between Jews and non-Jews are much less successful than is commonly recognized. Despite good intentions and a willingness to compromise in the early years, people change. Priorities change. Early agreements are re-evaluated or abandoned.

Studies have shown that intermarriages have significantly higher divorce rates and significantly lower marital satisfaction rates than same-faith marriages. Children of intermarriage are far less likely to grow up with confidence and strong self-esteem. The grandchildren of intermarriage almost never identify themselves as Jews — indeed in the vast majority of cases this already happens to adult children of intermarriage. Everyone hopes that their marriage will be the exception, yet very few are.

Sadly, this applies even in cases where all agreed that the child was to be raised as a "Jew only."

All of these points, discussed in detail within this book, are important to know and share. Yet, ultimately, arguments against intermarriage should be unnecessary. Being Jewish is a unique gift and a wonderful privilege. Being Jewish is a connection to the past and the future. Being Jewish is supposed to be — and can be — experienced as a delight: a life full of happiness, challenges, meaning, connections, learning, growth, spirituality, deep rituals, and joyful celebrations. Being Jewish can and should be a central and cherished part of our core identities. Once exposed to the depth and beauty of our heritage, wanting to marry another Jew is as natural as wanting to get married itself.

Appendices

Assimilation, Intermarriage, and Prime-Time Television

The funny thing about "the intermarriage question" is that in many ways, it is really a side point. Intermarriage is not an isolated phenomenon to be examined in a vacuum, but rather a predictable symptom of the much larger issue of assimilation.[1] Let us consider how assimilation and intermarriage are related.

Michael and Pam Radin are both Jewish, as are most of their close friends. They are not ashamed of their heritage; in fact they are quite proud of the people who produced Einstein, Seinfeld, and even Senator Joe, as they call him. They feel that their Jewish background has given them extra sensitivity to the underdog. They send their kids to Ivy League colleges. Like many of their peers, they don't belong to any Jewish organizations at all. Their health club is nearby, so they have no need for the Jewish Community Center's gym. And they don't bother joining a synagogue because they can buy tickets for the High Holidays. The Radins understand their Jewish identity as comprising ease with other Jewish people, sensitivity to the oppressed, and support for the State of Israel.

Their son, David, once explained to me how he came to marry out.

> *As I look back, being Jewish had almost nothing to do with our lives. We didn't hide the fact that we were Jewish, and we had lots of Jewish friends, but there was no substance to it. I couldn't have told you why it was important. My parents didn't know themselves. I got a paltry two hours a week of Jewish education until my bar mitzvah, when even that stopped. By the time I started dating, I didn't remember one idea, one song, or one word of Hebrew. Most of the girls I dated in high school were not Jewish, and there were never any problems because of it. When I met Sue at work, there weren't any particular differences keeping us apart. She knew nothing of her Catholic heritage and I knew less of my Jewish one. It is not hard to understand why I intermarried. Why wouldn't I have? She was beautiful, smart, and fun. There was chemistry. I didn't feel*

Jewish enough to think that intermarriage was an issue. As I look back, with the little Jewish content I had, it was bound to happen.

What we see from this story — which is typical of the majority of Jews who intermarry today — is that intermarriage is not an independent phenomenon that strikes randomly. It is actually a result of other realities of today's Jewish world. One outspoken critic of intermarriage, Conservative Rabbi Jack Moline from Alexandria, Virginia, wrote:

> The occurrence and high rate of intermarriage is not the root problem, but rather a symptom of something larger. The wider problem is that of a lack of substance in Jewish life, particularly in the more liberal approaches to Judaism (including our Conservative Movement).[2]

Similarly, Leonard Fine, a Reform Jewish writer and activist, said:

> I think the principle problem is not assimilation or intermarriage. It's boredom. The fact is that being Jewish is a boring experience for many Jews who are incapable of finishing this sentence: "It is important that Jews survive in order to...."[3]

When I ask students for their reflections on assimilation, they inevitably describe an upbringing similar to David's described above. There was no knowledge, joy, or passion about anything Jewish. Their Jewish lives lacked meaning and understanding.

In terms of formal Jewish education, most received none at all, and if they did it was boring and shallow. Such a framework is unlikely to produce knowledgeable, committed Jews. Furthermore, what little education they received ended at their bar/bat mitzvahs.

This last point is quite ironic. Early adolescence is when real questioning and thinking begins, so ending Jewish education then is entirely counterproductive. Similarly, the milestones of bar and bat mitzvahs are supposed to mark the beginning of real Jewish life. With many Jews today they mark the beginning of the end of Jewish education and involvement. Some modern rabbinic humor illustrates this point:

> The story is told of a Catholic priest, a Protestant minister, and a rabbi who were taking a walk. The priest laments that he can't get the pigeons out of his Church; the minister complains that he can't get rid of the mice. The rabbi confides that he managed to solve his pigeon and mouse problems. They ask how, and he explains, "I don't think it will help you, but one Saturday I got together all of the pigeons and the mice and bar mitzvahed them...and they never came back."

The joke is a funny, but sad, commentary on contemporary Jewish life. Jewish learning all too often ends in early adolescence. For many, intellectual development and Judaism have little to do with each other. While in reality, Judaism is an incredibly deep religion, philosophy, and culture, millions of Jews spend their entire adult lives relating to it with the perspective and background of an elementary school child. Not likely to inspire or impress an educated Ivy League mind, to say the least.

Self-Test

At the end of the day, how much does the average Jew know about Judaism? Try a simple self-test that may help clarify your level of Jewish knowledge: Ask yourself the following two questions:

(a) Who was Jesus' mother?

(b) Who was Moses' mother?

If you are typical of the average American Jew, chances are you knew that the answer to the first question is Mary. You probably did not know that the answer to the second question is Yocheved. While the test is a little unfair (Jesus' personality and family are more central to Christianity than Moses' are to Judaism), the point is significant nonetheless. Jews know little of their religion and culture, and many times know more about other philosophies and religions.

Think about it yourself: if you made a graph and needed to draw a line between knowledge of Judaism and intermarriage rates, how would it look? As I'm sure you guessed, the more knowledgeable a person is about Judaism, the less chance that they will intermarry.[4] After all, if a person doesn't know or care about their Jewishness, why be concerned with holding onto it? Why go to efforts to preserve something that means very little to you?

The point is that intermarriage is really only a symptom of the real culprit — the lack of Jewish knowledge and commitment on the part of the masses of Jews today. It is logical, then, that the real bulwark against intermarriage is Jewish literacy.

Unfortunately, Jewish literacy has declined tremendously over the last two generations.[5] Synagogue affiliation has dropped from 60% of American Jews to 40% in the last thirty-five years.[6] The number of Jewish children receiving a Jewish education has dropped from 602,000 in 1962 to 437,000 in 1990.[7] Jews know and do much less than they did even a generation ago.

Formal education aside, most Jews grow up today with little joy or passion about their Jewish identity. Are they really happy to be Jewish? Are you? We are supposed to enjoy our Jewishness. The belief system adds meaning to our lives. Shabbat and the holidays are times of such companionship, warmth, and pleasure that non-Jewish thinkers throughout the ages have envied them. The Jewish community adds connections to our lives. Identification with our past and our dreams for the future give depth to our existence in the world. Being Jewish is a wonderful, important, enjoyable gift. Yet so few know about it or enjoy it. That is the core problem. Intermarriage is nothing more than a result of that reality, albeit a major one.

Why Do People Assimilate?

Because assimilation has such a powerful impact on intermarriage, it is important for us to understand why Jews assimilate.

A century or two ago, the few Jews who assimilated into non-Jewish culture usually chose to do so deliberately. They often were tired of anti-Semitism. The oppression and limitations that often went along with being Jewish are hard for us to imagine today, but then they were quite real. For these Jews, who usually had little Jewish education, assimilation seemed to be the answer to their problems. Furthermore, access to wealth and social prestige was often blocked to Jews. The road to success ran through the Church courtyard. Whatever the reason, assimilation used to be a conscious choice.

Today, in most cases, assimilation usually "just happens," without any deliberate thought on the part of those involved. Despite the recent upsurge of anti-Semitism related to conflict in the Middle East, most American Jews live their lives without experiencing significant discrimination. And, as evidenced by the many successful Jews who are openly and actively Jewish (Senator Joe Lieberman, Dr. Laura Schlessinger, and Alan Dershowitz are recent famous examples, but there are countless others), a person no longer needs to assimilate into non-Jewish culture in order to "make it." We therefore need to ask the fundamental question: Why do Jews today assimilate? Consider the question for yourself and then compare your thoughts with what is written below. In my experience, reasons for assimilation will usually fall into the following categories.

- A lack of knowledge of Judaism. If a person knows little about something, it will likely be of little importance to him or her. Personally, I know next to nothing about the fine art of basket weaving. No offense to you basket-weavers, but it is basically irrelevant to my life. Do I care if the art is lost? Not particularly. Do I want it to be part of my life? No — why should I? What can it do for me? In the same way, a person who knows nothing about Judaism will rarely do anything to stay Jewish since it is about as important to them as basket weaving is to me, despite the greatness and beauty of the Jewish way of life. Their Jewishness is unlikely to last.

- Childish views of Judaism. Unfortunately, many Jews stopped their Jewish education when they were children or young adolescents. As Kirk Douglas put it, "If your education stopped at your bar mitzvah, then you're going through the rest of your life with a thirteen-year-old's view of Judaism. How tragic!" Many people are caught in this trap: since their minds have matured, they have rarely or never encountered the depth, beauty, and relevance of Judaism. Their intellectual thirst is quenched by politics, literature, or even other philosophies and religions. Because they think of Judaism with their childhood attitudes and understandings, they never take it seriously. They don't respect it. They are therefore unlikely to make efforts to counter nature's slide into majority culture.

• Negative experiences with the Jewish world. Perhaps some had a poor experience with Jewish education, which unfortunately turned them off. Or they knew someone "religious" who didn't live up to their expectations. Whatever the case, they experienced something that they didn't like and consciously and/or subconsciously they move away from Jewishness and towards assimilation.

• Avoiding latent anti-Semitism. As mentioned above, Jewishness is rarely a barrier to success in contemporary Western society. Yet, still today, a small number of people want to assure themselves that nothing will ever stand in their way. Since Judaism means relatively little to them, they don't feel it is worth taking any chances about latent anti-Semitism or being excluded from the old boy's network. They hide their Jewishness and attempt to leave it behind.

• Parents' nonverbal cues of what is important. Parents sometimes shoot themselves in the foot by claiming that being Jewish is important, but then doing things that run completely contrary to that claim, such as skipping Hebrew school for a matinee, when they would never allow skipping "regular school." Kids aren't stupid, and actions speak louder than words. They sense from their parents' priorities what is important — and what is not. If parents undermine the Jewish education of their kids, the road to Jewish identification in later life is uphill.

• Why *not* assimilate? My Italian-American neighbor isn't particularly worried about Italian-ness leaving his family, why should I be considered about Jewish-ness leaving my family?

• Psychological reasoning. Human beings like to fit into their surroundings. No one likes to stand out or feel different. In most places, immigrant populations do not last more than a generation or two, largely due to the innate human drive to fit in. People who live in areas with few Jews are unlikely to display their Jewishness, slowly allowing it to wither away.

Choices and Non-Choices

Whatever its causes, the reality of assimilation makes the intermarriage "question" quite easy to answer. Consider the following: When the first Europeans came to the Americas, they often made business deals with the Native Americans that seem incredible to us today. Huge amounts of natural resources were given away for a few trinkets. Large swaths of land were parted with for broken promises. Were the Native Americans naive? Had they never traded before? No — they were as intelligent as the

Europeans, and had bartered amongst themselves from time immemorial. However, they had never been overseas and simply did not know what commodities industrial European society needed and what prices the Europeans would really have paid for what they had to offer. Based on the little information they had, the decisions that they made seemed reasonable. However, in reality they didn't have the information necessary to make those decisions. They didn't know what great treasures lay in their backyards and ended up locking themselves into what were in retrospect some of the worst deals ever made.

If Jews who intermarried did so out of clear knowledge and foresight, our discussion would be quite different from what is presented in this book. But that is hardly ever the case. Those who intermarry are almost always those with the weakest Jewish identities of all, those who have no idea of what they are "throwing away." They are not actually *choosing* anything, since real choices require basic information on both sides of the issue. Whatever their particular reasons for assimilation, they simply don't know enough about Judaism to enable themselves to objectively weigh the risks of losing it.

A Little History

In order to further understand the phenomenon of modern assimilation, let us consider a little history. Up until the 1950s, the "melting pot" theme dominated America. Take a look at many American coins and you'll see the following Latin phrase: *E Pluribus Unum*. Its literal

translation is "From many, one." The United States is a
country of immigrants, and for generations its leaders understood that some kind of "Americanism" had to be created in order to build a unified people out of citizens
hailing from different lands and of varied cultures, religions, and beliefs. And indeed, many immigrants to
America wanted to adopt a new American identity. They
were fleeing poverty, war, and social stagnation in order
to come to the Golden Land where "your wits and your
brow" were what counted, not your ethnic background.
Many immigrants were quite happy to leave their "eth-
nicity" behind.

Jews — victimized throughout history — were especially prone to want to "just fit in." In their drive to become Americanized, many dropped all connections to
Jewish life. Some even changed their names to hide their
Jewish backgrounds. This led to some funny situations,
as some Jewish humor from the first half of twentieth
century America attests:

> A man calls up the lawyers' offices of Smith and
> Smith. "Can I speak with Mr. Smith, please?" he
> asks. "Which Smith do you want?" the secretary
> answers, "Rosenberg-Smith or Abramson-Smith?"

> An immigrant changed his name to Smith and
> then to Jones, so that when people heard his Yid-
> dish accent and asked him what his "old" name
> was, he'd be able to answer, "Smith!"

The humor of the day reflected the phenomenon of

"becoming American." For much of America's history, being American meant trying to fit in. The melting pot was the dominant ideal of the country. This whole period of American history was in fact anti-universalistic, as it openly encouraged the abandonment of sub-group cultures.

Respecting Roots

In the last thirty years, there has been a radical change in the mind-set of the United States. Ethnic identities have come back into vogue. There has been a massive change towards the acceptance of multiculturalism in America, which has emboldened many groups to hang on to their identities. For instance, I remember when Alex Haley's *Roots* was first broadcast in 1977, reaching 75% of American homes by the end of the miniseries. Its powerful black-identity message epitomized the black-is-beautiful revolution and pushed it forward. Being black was in. Being ethnic was in. The changes have been profound. We now speak of multiculturalism, pluralism, and the American mosaic. While unfortunately there is still much racism and prejudice around today, the tide has indeed turned. Most people have begun to see that ethnic and religious identities add to society's richness rather than detract from it. The universalistic ideal has become the norm.

Melt? — Yes. Intermarry? — No.

You might have thought that when the melting pot

ideal was in place, different subgroups would marry (and thus melt) into the majority culture at high rates, and now that multiculturalism is championed, the intermarriage rate would be lower. Yet, interestingly, the opposite is true!

Until a generation or two ago, the vast majority of people used to marry "their own kind." Intermarriage rates were historically very low. Catholics would marry Catholics. Protestants would marry Protestants. Jews would marry Jews. For various reasons (many of them are discussed in this book) people simply felt it was better that way. Despite the melting pot ideal, religion was different — a person was noble for hanging on to his or her religion. While some Jews completely abandoned Jewish identification, as mentioned above, many simply became more and more "Americanized" without intermarrying. Mixing religions in marriage had long been considered a bad idea.

You Are What You Watch

In our day, intermarriage rates across the board have skyrocketed. Almost without exception, subgroups today intermarry into the majority culture at high rates. Italians and Irish already experience out-marriage rates in excess of 60%, while Lutherans and Methodists marry outside their respective faiths at rates exceeding 70%.[8] Responding to the demographic trends, even the Catholics and Mormons have lessened their open opposition to intermarriage. Given this reality, it is hard to blame people for thinking that marrying "out of the faith" is acceptable and objecting to it is not.

After all, things have changed. When minorities were looked down upon, members from the majority wouldn't want to marry them. Even the minorities themselves often felt that the sociological differences were too deep to take the risk of intermarriage. Now, in addition to our new multicultural attitude, we live in a TV world. Television has been called the single most important teacher, parent, storyteller, and role model in America today. No matter how mature and educated we are, we are all deeply affected by what we watch. Billions of dollars are spent annually on advertising[9] because advertisers know that it is money well spent — the message will reach and influence millions of viewers.

One skeptic once said that Jews in the entertainment industry were the first to marry out and therefore created programming that would justify their actions and make their decisions more "normal" and "acceptable." Others suggest that the programming that they created — with its subtle pro-intermarriage themes — was simply a result of who they were, not maliciousness.

Whatever the explanation, the intermarriage obsession of television today is startling. In the mid-1990s I informally surveyed the obviously Jewish characters on prime-time television. There were eight. All of them, without exception, were intermarried or involved romantically with non-Jews. A few years later, the results of my informal survey were confirmed by observers in the field:

Among the many interfaith TV couples that include one Jewish partner are Paul Reiser's Jewish husband and Helen Hunt's Gentile wife, Jamie, on *Mad About You*; Miles Silverberg's romance with Corky on *Murphy Brown*; Jack Stein in love with the Waspy Wally Porter on *Love and War*; Marty Gold of *Anything but Love* in love with Hannah; Neil dating Gentile Alicia on *Flying Blind*; Stuart Markowitz of *L.A. Law* married to Wasp lawyer Anne Kelsey; Michael Stedman of *Thirtysomething* married to Hope, who is Protestant; Joel Fleishman of *Northern Exposure* consummating his feelings for Maggie O'Connell; David Silver dating Catholic Donna Martin, and his father married to Kelly Taylor's Wasp mom on *Beverly Hills 90210*, where the character Andrea Zuckerman married a Latino. On *Sisters*, the non-Jewish siblings Teddie and Frankie married Jewish men at different times. On *Dharma and Greg*, the Wasp Greg Montgomery married Dharma Finkelstein. Even *Brooklyn Bridge*'s eleven-year-old protagonist, Allen Silver, falls head over heels for the beautiful young Irish girl, Katie Monahan.

So pervasive has been the intermarriage and interdating on television that it has been virtually impossible to find a Jewish couple anywhere on the screen. When the intermarriage rate in the population at large hovers around 50 percent, on television it is well over 95 percent and growing.[10]

The results of this television model are enormous. Media deeply affects us. It shows happy images of inter-married people and rarely if ever mentions any associated problems. Intermarrying then enters our conscious and subconscious minds as problem-free. In fact, aside from all the classic reasons for assimilation mentioned above, in contemporary society intermarriage itself has subtly been presented as the normal, if not the ideal, type of marriage. No matter the realities of intermarriage that we have discussed, with nature's slide into majority culture and the influence of the television model, it is no wonder that intermarriage rates are so high.

Notes

1. In our context, assimilation can be defined as the weakening and eventual disappearance of Jewish identity from individuals, families, and communities as they merge into the majority culture that surrounds them.
2. Cited in Kagedan, *Intermarriage: What Can We Do? What Should We Do?*, 11.
3. *New York Magazine*, July 14, 1997.
4. See Phillips, *Re-examining Intermarriage*, for statistical information on this subject. While much research has been done on how many years and what type of Jewish education are "necessary" to avoid intermarriage, the relationship between Jewish knowledge and observance to intermarriage is very strong and undisputed. As Dr. Barack Fishman's recent study

puts it, "In line with data from the 1990 National Jewish Population Survey, the mixed-married Jews in our study received little or no Jewish education" (p. 73). Simply put, the more knowledge and the more observance, the less chance of intermarriage.

5. This fact is accurate for the American Jewish community as a whole; it does not apply to all communities.

6. Reported on jewishworldreview.com on January 11, 1999.

7. Ibid.

8. Jonathan D. Sarna, "Interreligious Marriage in America," in *Approaches to Intermarriage: Areas of Consensus*, American Jewish Committee, pp. 2–3. He mentions that both cultural and religious intermarriage rates have skyrocketed in the last two generations. In Seattle in 1960, 8% of native Japanese American men and 7% of the women married non-Japanese. In the same city in 1975, the rates were 43% and 49%. Today a substantial majority intermarry.

9. Aside from commercials, millions are spent just to have a favorite character reach for a particular bag of potato chips over another brand without ever mentioning a word. You can imagine what subtle messages and modes of thinking are being passed on to us on a regular basis. What we see on television greatly affects us.

10. In January 1999, the American Jewish Committee, the Annenberg School for Communications at the University of Southern California, and the Jewish Television Network convened a major conference with leaders of the television industry. The subject was "Jews in Prime-Time Television." Their report was published in 2000 jointly by the American Jewish Committee and the Norman Lear Center under the title *Television's Changing Image of American Jews*. The quote here is from Brandeis Professor Joyce Antler's article, "Problematics," in that report, p. 67.

Appendix 2

Quotations

I n this section you will find a collection of interesting and thought-provoking quotations from various sources on the subject of intermarriage.

And Abraham said to the senior servant of his household, that ruled over all he had..."I will make you swear by the Lord, the God of Heaven and the God of Earth, that you shall not take a wife for my son from the daughters of the Canaanites, among whom I dwell. But you shall go up to my country, and to my kindred, and take a wife for my son, for Isaac."

Genesis 24:2–4

Neither shall you make marriages with them: your daughter you shall not give to his son, nor his daughter shall you take for your son.

Deuteronomy 7:3–4

Every person who identifies as a Jew today should ask: "Ten, twenty, fifty years from now, who will stand in my place?"

> Antony Gordon and Richard Horowitz,
> "American Jews: An Endangered Species?"
> in *Jewish Spectator*, fall 1996, p. 381

How comfortable will you be lighting your Menorah that sits next to a nativity scene?

> Paul Silverman,
> *Staying Jewish and Surviving College*, p. 21

If the Nazi Holocaust, or the possibility of Jews again being slaughtered (in Israel, or elsewhere), or the disappearance of the Jewish people through assimilation affects you emotionally more than it does your non-Jewish friends, chances are that being Jewish means more, perhaps much more, to you than you think. And it is eminently possible that in the near future it will come to mean far more than at present.

> Dennis Prager and Joseph Telushkin,
> *The Nine Questions People Ask about Judaism*, p.149

Christian and Jewish attitudes towards intermarriage are very different. This is partially due to the fact that Jews are numerically small and dwindling, while Christians are not.

> Anonymous

Without an ideology, all we have to go on is a combination of vague pro-Israelism, nostalgia, fear of anti-Semitism, and liberal universalism that we dress up in Jewish garb.... You cannot expect continuity if Jews know little about what they wish to continue.... We are very good at telling the State Department what to do about Israel. But in the privacy of our homes, we cannot find the words to tell our children why they should be Jews.

Dr. Steven Bayme, Newsweek, July 1991

[Those who assimilate] are lost from Judaism, that is all.... Of course they survive as persons. But from the viewpoint of an army, it makes little difference whether a division is exterminated or disperses into the hills and shucks off its uniforms.

Herman Wouk, This Is My God, p. 234

We now have the data and studies to know that children who are left without an education leading to deep Jewish beliefs and practices have little chance of having Jewish descendants.

Viewpoint, Summer 1997/43

The difference isn't just between Moses and Christ. You're dealing with issues of money, sex, education, child-rearing practices, food, family relationships, styles of emotional expressiveness, issues of autonomy — all of these are culturally embedded.

Esther Perel, therapist

_____

By the third generation of intermarriage, Jewish identity has all but vanished. The chain, so well preserved over 150 generations, is broken.

Mark Winer and Aryeh Meir,
Questions Jewish Parents Ask about Intermarriage, p. 6

_____

Studies indicate that mixed-married families are far less likely to be involved in Jewish life than families in which both partners are Jewish, whether by birth or through conversion. Thus they are far less likely to join and attend synagogues, to become affiliated with Jewish organizations, to contribute to Jewish philanthropies, or to create a Jewish ambience in their homes. Significantly, they are half as likely to provide their children with a Jewish education...the intermarriage rate among children of intermarriage exceeds 90 percent. Second-generation intermarried families score very low on all measures of Jewish identity and are almost certain to be lost to the Jewish people.

Mark Winer and Aryeh Meir
Questions Jewish Parents Ask about Intermarriage, p. 19

_____

It seems to me worth asking if we have unintentionally helped create a climate in which intermarriage is increasingly taken for granted, accepted as normal and inevitable. By going out of our way to accept the intermarried, have we unwittingly conveyed the message that intermarriage is merely one option among equally valid family constellations? By working hard to make our synagogues safe environments for intermarried Jews, have we inadvertently become too comfortable with intermarriage?

Reform Rabbi Janet Marder,
in *Approaches to Intermarriage: Areas of Consensus*,
American Jewish Committee, p. 6

Appendix 3

Statistics

Intermarriage Rates

The following statistics were taken from the 1990 Natonal Jewish Population Survey:

- For every wedding between two Jews, two intermarriages take place.

- The intermarriage rate varies by geography (Denver 70%, Vancouver 75%); observance level and Jewish

Intermarriage Rates

1900–1920	2.0%
1921–1930	3.2%
1931–1940	3.0%
1941–1945	6.7%
1946–1950	6.7%
1956–1960	5.9%
1961–1966	17.4%
1966–1970	31.7%
1985–1990	52.0%

education (more education and observance, less intermarriage); and parents' married status (if parents are intermarried, 90% of kids intermarry; if both parents are Jewish, only about 40% of kids intermarry).

Out of 5.5 million U.S. Jews:

- 2 million Americans of Jewish "origin" do not identify themselves as Jews.

- 625,000 U.S. Jews are now practicing other religions. This accounts for over 10% of the American Jewish community.

- 1,000,000 American Jewish children under 18 are now being raised as non-Jews or with no religion. This accounts for 54% of all American Jewish children.

- 2 million self-identified Jews have no Jewish affiliations or connections whatsoever!

- When considering all married American Jews, 28% are married to non-Jews and 72% are married to other Jews (4% of these are converts).

- Statistically speaking, either you or your best friend will marry a non-Jew. Whichever one of you it is will have two children, both of them will intermarry, have two children also, and not one of the grandchildren will identify as a Jew.

Appendix 4

A Chapter for Parents

Many parents feel helpless in the face of a younger generation that is marrying out at unprecedented rates. Some parents who do prefer that their kids marry other Jews are afraid to voice their preferences — they have no desire to "rock the boat" by arguing, and don't feel competent to make their point clearly. So, good intentions notwithstanding, they say and do nothing. The chances that their kids will intermarry are high, but they feel powerless to stop it.

However, the truth is that parents do have a lot of influence in this area, and so I offer this chapter to parents. Here are some practical ways to increase the odds that your kids will marry other Jews. The earlier you start, the better.

Jewish Schools

The single best thing you can do to prevent your kids

from intermarrying is to send them to Jewish schools. Jewish schools create an informed, dedicated Jewish population. Some parents fear their kids will be isolated or handicapped by not going to the same schools that everyone else goes to, but the reality is otherwise. Jewish day schools score better on secular tests than other schools, and with a clarity and confidence in their Jewishness established early on, they easily learn to live alongside and respect other people. When day schools are not possible, "low intensity Jewish education which continues into the teen years reduces mixed marriage more effectively than a higher intensity Jewish education which stops at age thirteen."[1] Choose your Jewish school carefully – if the classes are boring and the teachers uninspired about being Jewish, you haven't achieved much by sending them. Also make sure not to undermine the school through words ("Hebrew school teachers can't get real jobs") or actions (missing Hebrew school for a movie when you'd never do so with "real" school). Kids will follow your lead.

Jewish Summer Camps, Youth Groups, etc.

Someone once said that the greatest gift America ever gave its children was the creation of summer camps. Kids look forward to camp all year. They daydream about it during school and write their camp friends letters when the teacher isn't looking. A good Jewish summer camp should accomplish two things: (a) Lifelong friendships are formed with other Jewish kids. Many teenagers renew these connections in college. Also, patterns of forming friendships with other Jews are also developed. (b) Kids experience a wonderful, happy Jewish life. They hold hands and dance for the Welcoming of Shabbat. They learn about holidays and speak some Hebrew. Wonderful teenage memories are associated with Jewish living.

Similarly, it is important to get kids involved in Jewish youth groups and activities. By creating venues for them to hang out with other Jews, their closest friends will naturally be Jewish.[2] Note that not all youth groups are equal: talk to the heads of your local chapter to make sure that their attitudes towards intermarriage mirror yours.

Live in a Jewish Neighborhood

In order to help create situations where the children's social networks will be Jewish, it is important to live in an area that has lots of Jewish people. Not only will they have Jewish kids to be friends with, but everything else that parents need to do (Jewish education, synagogue, cultural events, etc.) is much easier when there are many Jews around. If your kids are the only Jews they know, it is much harder to make them feel proud of their heritage. Statistically, bigger Jewish centers have much lower intermarriage rates than smaller Jewish centers.[3]

Be an Example

Let them see you learning about Judaism regularly — even once a week. Share what you are learning with them. Tell them how wonderful it is to be a Jew. Learn Torah, and let yourself be inspired by Jewish concepts and ideas, and the great things we have done for the world. If being Jewish is an important part of your daily life, and you have a good relationship with your children, they will usually follow in your footsteps. Note that simply paying synagogue membership fees or financially supporting Jewish causes without parents investing their own time and energy makes no impression whatsoever on children.[4]

Jewish Is as Jewish Does

The more Jewish a person feels and the more Jewish things he or she does, the more likely it is that they will want to marry someone with whom they can share their feelings and lifestyle. Starting as young as possible, bring children up with Jewish traditions as an important part of their lives. Celebrate Shabbat. Perhaps start with candle lighting and a nice family dinner on Friday night. Eventually, you can incorporate some easy and fun Jewish songs and activities (get yourself invited over to a family that celebrates Shabbat in order to learn what to do — it isn't as hard as you may think!). Prepare for the Passover Seder in order to make it fun and exciting for kids. Get a *pushke*, a charity box, and when it is full, get together as a family to decide which Jewish charity the money will go to. Read Jewish books with your kids, get some Jewish music, and put Jewish art on your walls (this can include pictures of Israel, traditional imagery from Europe, and much more). The more Jewish their home is growing up, the more you have created the "norm" for them, and the more they'll envision their future home to be that way too.

Jewish Stuff Is Different

When they've used up their allowance but want money for a Jewish book or other Jewish activity, do all you can to give it to them. Their Jewish youth group has a convention far away that they're dying to go to? Send them. They need a lift across town? If it is for something Jewish, take them. For Jewish activities and friends, go all out. When it comes down to your time and money, show them that Jewishness has first priority.

Let Them Know Who They Are

Kids like knowing where they come from. Get into your family's history, especially the Jewish aspects of it, and read up on Jewish genealogy and history. Tell them stories from the past. Let them know that they are part of something bigger than they are. That they belong, that they have a place. That they are heirs and transmitters of something special.

Travel Jewishly

When you travel, travel Jewishly. Visit Jewish tourist sites (you'd be surprised at how many there are). Bring Shabbat candles wherever you go, and use them. Frequent the local kosher restaurants. The unstated but powerful message is that being Jewish is not just something that we do at home or at synagogue. Rather, it is always with us. It is part of who we are wherever we are. Growing up this way will have huge effects on how the "kids" decide to live when they go to college and get their own apartments.

Send Them on Jewish Trips

Teenage trips to Eastern Europe and Israel have had amazing effects on the Jewish feelings of American teenagers. Furthermore, despite recent terrorism, many safe trips can still be planned. Start putting away money early and present these trips as a unique opportunity, something that they should look forward to and work towards. Arrange for former participants to tell them how great it was. Also, going to Israel yourself shows them what solidarity means, and that we are all one people. If you can, offer to pay for a Junior Year Abroad in Israel.

The College Life

When you help them choose a college, make sure that factors to consider include having a sizeable Jewish population and a vibrant Hillel and Chabad House. Four years is a long time, especially for the defining years of college. Who they become friends with and who they date will have an enormous impact on who they marry and who they become. Send them Jewish care packages at holiday times. Ideally, bring them home for Passover and other holidays — make them central family events. Call them to see where they will be going if they won't be with you. Let them know that one of your main concerns about their success at college is that they "stay Jewish."

Tell Them Openly that You Want Them to Marry Jewishly

Be direct and consistent about how important it is to you that they marry other Jews. Studies have found that when parents encourage kids to marry within the faith, they are much more likely to do so than when parents are silent on the issue.[5] While expressing your views does not guarantee that they will listen, it has more impact than many people think, especially when done with sincerity and respect. Parents have a responsibility to guide their children, to help them grow into contributing members of the planet, and to help them make good decisions. On important issues such as their marital happiness, your grandkids' identities, and your family's place in the Jewish people, you do have a role to play.

Read the "Dating" chapter in this book and consider if you will allow or approve of their dating non-Jews. See the "Dear Sean" letter at the end of this book for a good example of what to say on the subject. Buy or lend them *Why Marry Jewish?* Admit openly that they are adults and can make their own decisions, but suggest that they have all the information available to them before they make those decisions. And make sure they know that their decisions affect you and your entire family legacy.

If Your Child Is Already Dating a Non-Jew

The deeper the relationship is, the harder it is to break

it off. This is why it is crucial to set your kids up in situations where it will be easy to meet other Jews, and get them thinking about these issues before they meet that "special someone." However, there is still hope. One mother[6] became concerned that her daughter's relationship with a non-Jew was getting serious and began discussing the consequences of intermarriage. "Believe it or not," the mother said, surprise still lingering in her voice, "Amy and Carter had not talked about children. When they did, it turned out he didn't want his children to be Jewish. The relationship ended."

Notes

1. Phillips, *Re-examining Intermarriage*, p. 17.

2. In fact, the existence of Jewish friendship circles in teenage years seems to be the single biggest predictor of Jewish friendship circles later in life, which itself is a major predictor of intermarriage. Dr. Sylvia Barack Fishman's study, "Jewish and Something Else," found that of Jews who as teenagers had mostly non-Jewish friends, 68% continued that pattern in college, and only 9% had mostly Jewish friends in college. Yet of Jews who as teenagers had mostly Jewish friends, 87% had friendship circles in college that were mixed, mostly, or all Jewish. Only 13% had mostly non-Jewish friendship circles. The point is that teenage friendship patterns are crucial to future friendship patterns, and thus intermarriage.

3. One study found that the intermarriage rate for New York is "half that of the rest of country" (New York Jewish Population Survey, p. 101, table 4:1, using "perfect cases"). Another study found that intermarriage rates in Denver and Phoenix are 1.5 and 1.4 times as high as Los Angeles (Bruce Phillips, "*Factors Associated with Intermarriage: A Preliminary Investigation*," HUC-Jewish Institute of Religion, LA,

World Congress of Jewish Studies.)
4. Phillips, *Re-examining Intermarriage*, p. 13.
5. Fishman, "Jewish and Something Else," p. 104 table 20: 62% of Jews who married other Jews reported that their parents had discouraged intermarriage, while only 33% of Jews who intermarried said so. As widely reported at the time, only 5% reported a "backlash" effect where parental discouragement of intermarriage had negative reactions.
6. Described in *The Jewish Journal of Greater Los Angeles*, December 24, 1999.

Bibliography

Cowan, Paul and Rachel. *Mixed Blessings*. Penguin Books, 1989.

Dershowitz, Alan. *The Vanishing American Jew*. Little Brown, 1997.

Fishman, Sylvia Barack. "Jewish and Something Else: A Study of Mixed-Marriage Families." William Petschek National Jewish Family Center of the American Jewish Committee, released internationally in May 2001.

Kagedan, Tom, ed. *Intermarriage: What Can We Do? What Should We Do?* United Synagogue of Conservative Judaism Publications, 1992.

Johnson, Paul. *A History of the Jews*. Weidenfeld and Nicolson, 1987.

Kornbluth, Doron, ed. *Jewish Matters*. Southfield, Mich.: Targum Press, 1999.

Larson, Jeffry. *Should We Stay Together?* Jossey-Barr, 2000.

Mayer, Egon. *Children of Intermarriage: A Study in Patterns of Identification and Family Life.* American Jewish Committee, 1983.

McManus, M. *Marriage Savers.* Grand Rapids: Zondervan Publishers, 1993.

Medding, Peter, Gary Tobin, Sylvia Barack Fishman, and Mordechai Rimor. *Jewish Identity in Conversionary and Mixed Marriages.* New York: American Jewish Committee, 1992.

Petsonk, Judy, and Jim Remsen. *The Intermarriage Handbook.* New York: Quill, 1991.

Prager, Dennis, and Joseph Telushkin. *The Nine Questions People Ask about Judaism.* Touchstone, 1986.

Phillips, Bruce A. *Re-examining Intermarriage: Trends, Textures, Strategies.* American Jewish Committee and the Wilstein Institute, 1997.

Sales, Amy. *Values and Concerns of American Jewish Youth: JCC Maccabi Teen Survey.* Cohen Center for Modern Jewish Studies, 1994.

Silverman, Paul. *Staying Jewish and Surviving College.*

Sklar, Marshall. *American's Jews.* New York: Random House, 1971.

Spiro, Ken. *WorldPerfect.* Simcha Press, 2002.

Winer, Mark, and Aryeh Meir. *Questions Jewish Parents Ask About Intermarriage.* American Jewish Committee, 1992.

Wouk, Herman. *This Is My God.* N.Y.: Little Brown, 1959.

Postcript

Dear Sean

Dear Sean,

I know this might sound strange coming from a father who's far from a religious Jew, but now that you're dating, there's something I need you to understand. The single most important decision you'll ever make in life will not be about your education or career. It will be whom you marry. Because who your wife will be will determine, more than anything else in your adult life, the person you become, the family you'll raise, what you'll leave on earth when it will be time to go. I know the end of life isn't something you probably give much thought to. Not many of us do, at least not until we became sick or old enough to see it hovering on the horizon. But a final day does arrive, sooner or later, for each of us. And when it comes, very few of the things we thought made such a big difference will seem to matter at all. And other things we

---

Author's note: this letter has been circulating around the Jewish world for some time. I don't know who the author is, but it speaks for itself. Please inform me if you know of its origin.

didn't bother to give much thought to will suddenly loom very large. We'll want to look back at our lives and feel that, in those areas, we pretty much did the right thing.

Sean, the right thing for a Jewish person is to marry another Jew. Not only because our religion requires it, which it does. But when Jews "marry out," they disrespect who they are, they are disloyal to the Jewish past, and they chip away at the Jewish future. Whether or not our family kept strictly kosher or observed the Sabbath or attended services often enough is all one thing. But the thought of bringing about the end of a proud Jewish line stretching back in time for centuries is another. It's more than a religious transgression. It's a betrayal.

You never asked to be a Jew, that's true. You were born one. But that identity is not a burden. It's a gift. It means you are part of something bigger, much bigger than yourself. Each of us Jews is the culmination of the hopes of hundreds of Jewish ancestors. Don't forget, you're not just Sean, you're Shmuel. And even if you only use your Jewish name when you get called to the Torah, it is still who you really are, an inheritance from your grandfather, and to him from an ancestor of his. You can't just ignore the meaning of something like that. It's a deep responsibility. All of my ancestors and your mother's, all those Jews who came before us, lived their lives — and sometimes willingly gave them up — to preserve their Jewish identity and heritage.

Yes, I know, love is a powerful emotion. That's exactly why I'm writing this as you begin to date. The young women you become close to will form the pool from which you will choose a life-mate. Don't give yourself the opportunity to fall in love with someone you cannot, as a Jew in good conscience, marry. And never forget that what the world calls "love" is not all there is to a successful and happy life. Every marriage that ended in divorce or worse, after all, was born in a rush of love. For a marriage to truly work, there must be not only attraction and mutual care but shared ideals and goals. And part of a Jewish man or woman's goals should be an embrace of their Jewish identity, and the instilling of that identity into their children. I don't care whether the girl you marry is white, black, or yellow, or if she speaks English, Hebrew, Yiddish, or Swahili. I don't care if she was born a Jew or became one, legally, properly, and out of sincere conviction. But if she isn't Jewish, I know there will be tears, in your mother's eyes and mine — and also in heaven.

They say these days that most Jewish parents in America don't care if their children marry other Jews or not. I hope it's not true, but even if it is, remember what I always told you: Being a Jew means being ready to buck the tide, to say no to others — even to many others — when something important is at stake. Sean, you're my legacy to the future. May you always have the courage and the strength to do the right thing.

Love,

Dad

LOOKING FOR JEWISH KNOWLEDGE AND INSPIRATION?

JEWISH MATTERS:

A Pocketbook of Knowledge and Inspiration
Edited by Doron Kornbluth

Half a century ago, the Jewish People and its traditions were pronounced dead. Yet today, more and more Jews from across the spectrum of religious practice want to learn about their heritage. In this slim volume, twenty-three of the most insightful and profound Jewish leaders, thinkers and educators in the Jewish world today offer their knowledge and inspiration on topics as varied as relationships, prayer, mysticism, and happiness.

Authors include: Lisa Aiken, Mordechai Becher, Natan Lopes Cardozo, Dovid Gottlieb, Tziporah Heller, Leah Kohn, Lawrence Kelemen, Gila Manolson, Dovid Orlofsky, Gerald Schroeder, Rivkah Slonim, Ken Spiro, and more.

Twenty-three essays worth reading –
because being Jewish matters.

JEWISH WOMEN SPEAK
ABOUT JEWISH MATTERS

Edited by Sarah Kornbluth and Doron Kornbluth

Women and Spirituality. Women and Prayer. Great Jewish Women, Past and Present. Marriage. Motherhood. Career Choices. Authentic Voices of Jewish Women Today.

Including articles by the most respected and interesting women in Jewish education today: Tehilla Abramov, Lisa Aiken, Tziporah Heller, Dr. Liz Kaufman, Leah Kohn, Gila Manolson, Lori Palatnik, Sarah Yocheved Rigler, Feige Twerski, Denah Weinberg and more.

Because when Jewish Women Speak –
it's worth listening!

Author and speaker Doron Kornbluth gives entertaining, inter-active, and though-provoking seminars and lectures all over the world. His most famous talks related to this book are:

- KIDS LOVE BEING JEWISH:
  Instilling Jewish Pride and Joy into Your Family

- THE SECRET:
  Strengthening Your Kids' Jewish Future

- LOVE, DATING & RELIGION:
  An Interactive Seminar for Jewish Singles

- TALKING ABOUT INTERMARRIAGE:
  Tools for Parents and Grandparents

- TEENAGE JEWISH PRIDE SEMINAR:
  Who Are We & Who Am I?

"Kornbluth's lecture hit a chord..."
Vancouver Jewish Independent

"This was a fabulous event and we got terrific feedback. I highly recommend it to other JCC's."
David A. Kirschtel
Executive Director, JCC-Y of Rockland, NY

www.doronkornbluth.com
info@doronkornbluth.com

We're interested in your comments.

How did you like the book? How did it affect you?

What are your experiences, questions and comments about interfaith relationships?

info@doronkornbluth.com